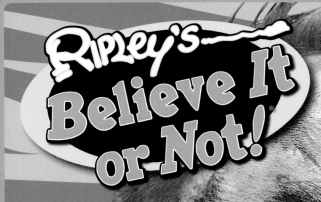

Believe It or Not!®

SPECIAL EDITION 2011

SCHOLASTIC INC.
NEW YORK · TORONTO · LONDON · AUCKLAND
SYDNEY · MEXICO CITY · NEW DELHI · HONG KONG

ISBN 978-0-545-23800-7

PUBLISHING

Developed and produced by Ripley Publishing Ltd

Publishing Director: Anne Marshall
Art Director: Sam South
Editorial Director: Becky Miles

Project Editor: Rosie Alexander
Picture Researcher: James Proud
Editorial Assistant: Charlotte Howell
Designer: Rocket Design
Indexer: Hilary Bird
Reprographics: Juice Creative

12 11 10 9 8 7 6 5 4 3 2 1   10 11 12 13 14 15/0
                                              82

Printed in China
Lenticular is printed in the U.S.A.
First printing, September 2010

Contents

P.32 ▶▶

P.84 ▶▶

P.104 ▶▶

◀◀ P.94

Introducing...
Robert Ripley

It was in 1918, while working as a cartoonist on the *New York Globe*, that Robert Ripley first became fascinated by what he termed the "curioddities" of life—the world's amazing feats and folk, artifacts, and accounts. A stylish, energetic figure, immaculately dressed in suit and spats (a cloth covering for shoes), or safari shirt and hat, his interest sparked a lifelong obsession—to scour the globe and record his findings in the daily column he produced for the newspaper.

Called *Ripley's Believe It or Not!* the column openly encouraged readers to write in with obscure material and photographs, and up to 3,500 letters unceremoniously dropped onto his desk every day. That some of them reached his offices at all was a reflection of Robert Ripley's immense popularity and fame. One envelope arrived unaddressed, scribbled instead with just the words "Believe It or Not!" Others had the address written in code. Another had just a rip on the corner to indicate "Rip"-ley. A hand-drawn boat and ripple-y water got there too.

By 1933, Robert Ripley had collected such a vast quantity of material that he was able to open his first Believe It or Not! museum (Odditorium) in Chicago, in which he could showcase it all. So startling was each exhibit, that, Ripley reported, "One hundred people fainted every day and we had to have six beds."

Visiting 201 countries and notching up over 464,000 miles, Ripley ploughed on with his search, and, today, there are 31 such museums in 11 countries. The collections are constantly being expanded. Recently, Ripley's acquired crickets painted to resemble Michael Jackson, a six-foot-tall rubber band ball weighing more than 9,000 pounds, and many more.

If you have a strange fact, contact www.ripleybooks.com, or write to BION Research, Ripley Entertainment Inc., 7576 Kingspointe Parkway, 188, Orlando, Florida, 32819.

Although not always holding a shrunken head, as below, Ripley broadcast a weekly radio show for 14 years, often reporting from the strangest locations—a rattlesnake pit, a shark tank, miles underground in a cave, or mid-sky as he parachuted from a plane. So much of a celebrity was he that, when he died in 1949, thousands lined the streets of New York to watch his coffin pass by.

Ripley comes face-to-face with a giant Japanese spider crab, which has eight legs, each of which can grow to four feet.

"I venture to say that I've been called a liar more than anyone else in the world. I enjoy being called a liar. I don't blame anyone for thinking me one, because there's nothing stranger than the truth." Robert Ripley

Page 85

Be honest, don't you tire of the humdrum parts of life, the run of the mill, the average? Most of us wish at some time or other to stand up, do something different, become famous even.

Some members of the human race actively go looking for fame and attract attention with fabulously freakish, dangerously dynamic feats. Others struggle on, against all the odds, purely for a sense of personal achievement. A lucky few have fame thrust upon them, because what they can do naturally is wonderfully unusual.

So, three cheers for them all! Ripley's celebrates them here! Over the following pages, you will "ooh" and "aah" over the eye-popping images and are free to soak up the thousands of bits of information, each one strange but true. Try making a list of your top ten stories. Maybe you'll include the eight-toed foot, the 39-inch car, or the couple who opted for a Shrek-themed wedding. Or the pint-sized meal. Take your pick. Every single one is a show-stopper.

MIND BOGGLER!

Keep an eye out for bite-sized, shocking facts in the Mind Bogglers. They'll provide just enough information to leave you open-mouthed.

Page 95

Page 105

Ripley's Archive

Some of the black-and-white images in this book are taken from the vast Ripley's Archive. Robert Ripley produced the photographs as cartoons for his column. The BION cartoons are still produced on a daily basis, making it the longest-running syndicated cartoon in the world.

RIPLEY'S ARCHIVE

Page 46

Page 39

"It's a pretty good little old world after all, don't you think?"
Robert Ripley

chapter one

Life As You
Don't

Know It

Like Nothing on Earth

Cool Colors

Not every iceberg is the same color. Some icebergs look white because the frozen water contains tiny air bubbles. If the water melts and refreezes, forming solid ice, the bubble-free ice appears blue. Sometimes the ice picks up layers of dust, soil, or algae, which can form multicolored candy stripes across the center of the 'berg.

Rock On!

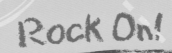

Keen-eyed Google Earthers have discovered all kinds of weird formations and other oddities. This face, spotted in Alberta, Canada, is a drainage feature created by the erosion of soft clay, and has been christened the Badlands Guardian. He seems to be wearing Native American headdress and earphones (which are actually a road leading to an oil well). Could he be listening to rock music?

Stony Sea

Imagine finding a field of rocks floating in the ocean. That's what confronted Swedish yachtsmen Fredrik Fransson and Hakan Larsson as they sailed from San Francisco, California, to Australia. The huge island of pumice was created by a volcanic eruption near the Pacific islands of Tonga in 2006. Rafts of this light rock can travel great distances and transport creatures such as crabs and barnacles across the ocean. After the gigantic Krakatoa eruption in 1883, giant pumice rafts carried human skeletons all the way to Africa. The new volcanic island is expected to disappear within ten years.

JUST ASKING...

When did you first spot the island?

"We left Neiafu in the northern part of Tonga on August 11, 2006, sailing toward Fiji. Soon we discovered brown, grainy streaks in the water. As we got farther, the streaks turned into heavy bands of floating matter, until the whole horizon was a solid line that looked like a desert."

Were you able to sail through the pumice?

"When we entered the solid field, it started to pile up and behaved like wet concrete. The sight was unbelievable; it looked like rolling sand dunes as far as the eye could see. Our speed went from seven knots to one knot as the pumice stones dragged along the waterline. We turned around as quickly as we could and headed toward clear water."

How did you cross the pumice to reach your destination?

"We motored out early the next morning and sailed along the pumice rafts until they were so broken up that we could safely steer through them. We collected a few stones, some as big as a soccer ball."

Location Location

Playing Safe?

Enthusiasts celebrated Scrabble's 60th anniversary in November 2008 by playing the word game in some stunning locations. Some played their moves at 13,000 feet for example, after throwing themselves out of a plane. Others set the board down with alligators just a few feet away. Two gamekeepers in the Lion Park, Lanseria, South Africa, had a game in the company of overexcited lionesses. Concentration, as always with Scrabble, was important.

MIND BOGGLER!

CONTINENTAL DRIFT
Because of movements in the Earth's crust, America and Europe are moving apart by just over an inch a year—about the same speed as a human fingernail grows.

Epic Splash

Brrrrrr!

A swimming pool in London, England, was transformed into the North Atlantic Ocean for a special screening of the Oscar-winning movie, *Titanic*. Movie fans wearing period costume took to the lifeboats as they floated in a sea of icebergs. All survived the experience, but they may have been more than a little stiff by the end of the 3-hour-12-minute film.

Crash Pad

It may look like a disaster in the jungle, but high-flying vacationers will feel right at home in this Costa Rican hotel. It took five large trucks to transport the 1965 Boeing 727 to the rainforest resort, where it was fitted out as a luxury, two-bedroom suite. Balconies on each wing offer treetop views, so you could find yourself eye-to-eye with toucans, sloths, and monkeys.

Hanging by a Hair

Precariously perched at the top of a cliff, the gravity-defying Golden Rock is one of the most sacred places in Myanmar (Burma). Pilgrims apply squares of gold leaf to the granite boulder. According to legend, this head-shaped rock is held in place by a strand of the Buddha's hair, given to the king by a hermit.

Tricks and Mortar

House on Its Head

Polish partners Klausdiusz Golos and Sebastian Mikiciuk have designed an upside-down house on the north German island of Usedom as part of a project called "The World on Its Head." Unlike other topsy-turvy houses, all the furniture and fittings (except the stairs) are upside down too. The house was intended to attract tourists, but visitors have complained of feeling dizzy and seasick once inside.

MIND BOGGLER!

RAPID REBUILD
The day after a tornado tore through Chris Graber's home in Missouri, his family was settling into their new house—rebuilt in just 15 hours by their kind Amish neighbors.

Grand Illusion

The design of the Australian Customs Service building in Melbourne, Australia, is based on the well-known "café wall illusion" that is produced by dark and light rectangles arranged in a zigzag pattern. Believe it or not, the orange lines are parallel and an equal distance apart. This illusion works best when the horizontal lines are a color that is midway between the light and dark panels.

All in One Piece

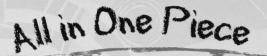

Tornadoes can tear down buildings, rip up trees, and toss vehicles like toys, so when a tornado hits a house and demolishes a whole wall, you would expect almost everything inside to be destroyed. Imagine this couple's surprise, therefore, when they found that their dishes hadn't just survived the twister, they were still neatly arranged on their shelves.

Leaning Tower of Suurhusen

Forget the Leaning Tower of Pisa. A late-medieval church tower in the north German village of Suurhusen is leaning over at an angle of 5.19 degrees, topping the tilt of the Italian tower by 1.22 degrees. The church was built on oak foundations, which rotted over time, causing the tower to sink on one side.

Wheely Good

Car Crusher

Twice the length of a family sedan and weighing more than a bus, this beast of a bike was built by Australian stunt driver Ray Baumann. The bike is powered by a truck engine, and the giant wheels are taken from a digger. The monster motorbike displays its awesome abilities at stunt shows, where it flattens cars and caravans like soda cans.

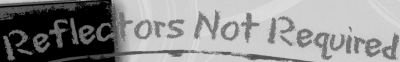

Reflectors Not Required

British designer Ben Wilson has brought a touch of bling to the humble bicycle with this glittering lowrider, encrusted with almost 110,000 Swarovski crystals. Inspired by a trip to Hollywood, the bike would be perfect for an environmentally friendly superstar. But at $50,000, it would need a heavy-duty security lock.

Rough Ride

Joff Summerfield is the second man to have ridden around the world on a penny-farthing—the first being fellow Brit Thomas Stevens in 1887. The former Formula 1 engineer, who built the replica Victorian penny-farthing himself, averaged 11 mph during his two-and-a-half-year trip. He covered 21,976 miles, visited 23 countries, and survived being mugged, hit by two trucks, and sharing a campsite with crocodiles.

LEAP TO IT!
Fast pedal to page 94 to find a bike you can carry in the palm of your hand.

Wacky Wheels

Since their invention some 5,500 years ago, wheels have been round.

But a Chinese inventor was inspired to remodel the classic design while rolling a triangular pencil on his desk. The front wheel of Guan Baihua's innovative bike is a pentagon, while the back is triangular. Apparently, the ride is surprisingly smooth, although pedaling is harder than usual.

Ouch!

Beijing 2008

ROCKET
BOAN BIKE

Rhett Dashwood has transformed topography into typography by creating the first Google Earth alphabet. It took the Melbourne designer six months to find all the letters in his home state of Victoria, Australia. Letter landmarks include the Kooyong tennis courts (C), Patterson Lakes marina (G), and Melbourne Cricket Ground (O).

Aerial Alphabet

CarriedAway

Stick Stack

Why make two journeys, when one will do? This well-camouflaged Chinese three-wheeler could be taking part in a big-hair competition. The huge, precariously balanced load of sticks leaves little room for other road-users as the truck wobbles its way through the streets of Jining City, China.

Loony Load

Transporting a trike on a car is possible, but the reverse is not a great idea. Police in Anhui Province, China, agreed and issued this driver a ticket as he tried to carry the burned-out shell of a car on the back of his tricycle. Perhaps next time, he'll consider using a flatbed truck.

Travelers approaching these two cyclists struggling along a road in Vietnam might think they were headed toward a couple of giant porcupines. In fact, the cyclists are transporting towering stacks of shrimp traps to sell at a local market. Village women weave the basketwork traps using strips of bamboo.

MEGA MOVERS

★ Traveling at just one mile per hour, NASA's six-million-pound crawler vehicle takes five hours and 1,000 gallons of fuel to move the space shuttle from the assembly building to its launch pad.

★ Giant earthmovers used in the mining industry are the size of a two-story house, with tires twice the height of an adult male. These vehicles carry more than 300 tons and weigh as much as 190 cars.

★ Reverend Kevin Fast pulled an International Loadstar truck weighing 126,292 pounds more than 137 feet. The minister from Ontario had previously pulled three fire trucks weighing a total of 102,933 pounds more than 100 feet.

LEAP TO IT! Check out page 77 to see how a robot suit can carry a paralyzed climber up a mountain.

All Aboard

Commuters on crowded trains should consider themselves lucky. This train carrying Sunni Muslims home after a religious gathering in Multan, Pakistan, takes overcrowding to the extreme. Hundreds of thousands of devotees from all over the country attended the annual event—and most seem to be taking the same train home.

Green Gauge
Potato Power

ZAP!

The ingredients for this sculpture by Czech artist Kristof Kintera are 660 pounds of potatoes, 250 pairs of zinc and copper electrodes, a microchip controller, LCD displays, and digital watches. Entitled "We've Got the Power!", the art installation is a giant battery, with each potato producing almost one volt. Like an ordinary battery, it converts chemical energy into electrical energy. The potato acts as a conductor and keeps the zinc and copper separate, so that the electrons in the copper are forced to move. This creates a flow of electricity.

Thirsty Work

Buddhist monks from Khun Han, Thailand, have recycled more than one million empty bottles by using them to build a temple and a complex of buildings including prayer rooms, a hall, a water tower, tourist bathrooms, and several small bungalows. The bottle caps did not go to waste either—they have been used to create decorative mosaics of Buddha.

ECO FACT FILE

⭐ The aluminum foil used to wrap a day's output of Hershey's Kisses would cover almost 40 football fields. All that foil is recyclable.

⭐ The average American uses seven trees a year in paper, wood, and other products. This adds up to about 2,000,000,000 trees per year.

⭐ Each ton of recycled paper saves 17 trees, 79 gallons of oil, 7,000 gallons of water, 41,000 kilowatts of energy, 60 gallons of air pollution, and three cubic yards of landfill space.

⭐ Every month, we throw out enough recyclable glass bottles and jars to fill a giant skyscraper.

⭐ Every three months, Americans throw away enough aluminum to rebuild the whole U.S. commercial air fleet.

TINY WASTE

The average American discards 1,700 pounds of trash each year, whereas Dave threw away only:

Trash: 30.5 pounds
Cardboard: 19 pounds
Plastic bags: 4 pounds
E-waste: 12 pounds
Miscellaneous recycling: 26.5 pounds
Paper: 69.5 pounds
9 pizza boxes
11 drink cartons
153 glass bottles
14 cups
2 aluminum cans
64 plastic bottles and jugs
8 plastic yogurt tubs with tops
8 old paint cans

Refuse Reduction

In 2008, Dave Chameides, also known as Sustainable Dave, didn't put out a single piece of trash—instead he stored it in his Los Angeles basement. Dave enlisted the help of some worms to eat his leftover food and waste paper. And by avoiding excess packaging, plastic bags, and bottled water, he managed to reduce his garbage for one year to what the average American creates in six days.

Shake Up

In 2007, a powerful earthquake close to the Solomon Islands lifted Ranongga Island by 10 feet, pushed coral reefs out of the water, and tossed up the wreckage of a World War II torpedo boat.

POISON

TUNNEL TOWN

A copper mine deep inside the mountains of the Chilean Andes has more than 1,500 miles of underground tunnels, along with its own train station, restaurants, and medical facilities.

FRUIT FINDS...

Archaeologists in Japan have found a melon well past its sell-by date, yet the 2,100-year-old fruit still has flesh on its rind. At 2,600 years old, a cherry unearthed from Loch Tay, Scotland, is even more ancient, but it still has its flesh. Both fruits were preserved in mud, which protected them from attack by micro-organisms.

Worm Shower

Residents of Jennings, Louisiana, were shocked to see tangled clumps of live worms falling from the sky. The worms were probably sucked up by a waterspout five miles away, then dropped on the town.

CRYSTAL KINGDOM

Nearly a thousand feet beneath the Chihuahuan Desert in Mexico lies a cave filled with crystals the size of trees. The crystals may look icy, but the temperature in the Cueva de los Cristales is a sweltering 130°F, with 90–100 percent humidity. The cave is warmed by magma and, because of the heat, minerals in the groundwater were converted to gypsum, which formed the giant crystals.

Weighty Issue

Visitors to certain areas of Canada may get a surprise if they step on the scales when on vacation. A large area in the north of the country has lower gravity than the rest of the world, so people weigh slightly less there.

DARK DAYS

Founded in the 14th century, Rattenberg, Austria, was built in the shadow of the Rat Mountain to shield it from invaders. Protection came at a price, however, and the town is one of the few places far from the poles that receives no direct sunlight in winter. Now there are plans to install 15 mirrors to reflect the sun during the dark months.

DINO DISCOVERY

Normally only the hard parts of a body such as bones and teeth are fossilized, but the remains of a duck-billed dinosaur discovered in Montana include skin, muscle, and even traces of pollen from its last meal.

-6 V 79

METRO
178
VENTAS
IDA Y VUELTA
O FESTIVO

UTILIZACION
SEGUN TARIFAS

TuckIn

Seal Flipper Pie

Check out this unusual traditional recipe from Newfoundland, Canada. The pie is often enjoyed at Easter time.

Seal Flipper Pie

...Serves four

Soak four seal flippers in water with 1 tsp baking soda for half an hour.

Dip in seasoned flour and fry in pork fat.

Add two chopped onions.

Mix 1 tsp flour with a cup of water and 1 tsp Worcestershire sauce. Pour over the flippers and bake in a moderate oven for two to three hours.

Cover with pastry and bake for another half an hour.

Hmm... tasty

Make It Snappy

It's hard to say whether this lizard is slipping his arm round his friend for a bit of comfort, just before he heads between the lips of Thai farm employee Somsak Inta. What is clear, though, is that Somsak has been eating house lizards for twenty years, as a means of treating health problems that he claims could not be cured by modern medicine.

Yum Yum

Rats are a delicacy in parts of Asia. Once a food only for the poor, rat meat is now more expensive and more highly prized than pork or chicken. Most of the rats live in rice-paddy fields, so farmers are pleased to get rid of the rice-eating rodents. Other Far Eastern favorites include tarantulas, lizards, snakes, crickets, and bats.

Thieves Beware

Fool sandwich stealers with these anti-theft lunch bags printed with moldy green splotches. No more need to keep your BLT under lock and key—would-be thieves will assume that your sandwich is long past its sell-by date. If nothing else, it will gross out your friends when you open your lunchbox.

Odd Eggs

Croatian poultry farmer Stipa Gregacevic was amazed when his prize black hen started to lay green eggs. "I can't really explain why it happens," said Stipa. "Some say it might be because we put red pepper in the hen food." Whatever the reason, customers are happy to shell out twice as much for the unusual eggs.

Way to Go

Crouching Coffin

Paseka Hlatshwayo may have solved the problem of overcrowded cemeteries. Historically, it was normal for people to be buried in a crouching position in Africa, so the medical student from South Africa came up with a coffin designed to accommodate a squatting body. The space-saving casket requires a burial plot just one-third the normal size.

MIND BOGGLER!

R.I.P. – UP A TREE
Instead of burying the dead under the ground, a number of indigenous tribes place them high up in a tree.

Woaaah!

Dying to Play

Ahlgrim's Acres in Palatine, Illinois, puts the "fun" into funeral. The funeral home's standard package includes an optional round of miniature golf, played on the nine-hole course in the basement. Obstacles include coffins, skulls, headstones, and a mummy, while recorded screams and spooky music create a creepy atmosphere. The basement also offers Ping-Pong and Foosball tables, shuffleboard, and video games.

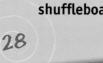

28

High-Tech Headstone

Headstones have been carved from marble or granite for hundreds of years, but now an Austrian company has designed a grave for the 21st century. Solar cells, arranged in the shape of a cross, power a glowing gravestone and a digital display, which can be programmed with details of the deceased and personal blessings. Unlike engraved stone, this memorial can be updated at any time.

Ashes to Art

Mother of one, Mrs. Filkins from Bradley, North Yorkshire, decided to turn her husband's death in 2008 into something beautiful and use his ashes to make a piece of art. She chose a landscape oil painting of the couple's last holiday to Menorca, Spain, to remember her husband by. Painted by artist Val Thompson, from Sunderland, County Durham, who specializes in incorporating ashes into paintings, Mr. Filkins's ashes were used alongside oil paints to create the cherished masterpiece.

ONE-LINER
Taphephobia is the fear of being buried alive.

chapter two

Odd-inary Folk

Airplay

Hit the High Note

Musicians often get carried away when they play, but Joja Wendt took music to new heights when he attached his piano to a hot-air balloon. True to his motto "playing the piano is fun," the pianist from Hamburg, Germany, took to the sky to perform Tchaikovsky's *Dance of the Sugar-Plum Fairy* as he floated above Wolfgang Lake in Austria.

Diamond Dive

Following seven years' planning and training, 100 skydivers from 14 countries linked up over Lake Wales, Florida, to create a diamond formation the size of a jumbo jet. The jumpers were released in four separate drops by five planes and held the formation for 12 seconds. Falling at 1,200 feet per minute, they had just 11 minutes between the first drop and reaching the ground.

Hold on Tight

Greg Gasson has a day job as a software engineer—and an exciting second life as one of the world's most accomplished skydivers.

Those who find the thought of parachuting out of a plane in the typical way a little boring might enjoy this shot of Greg hanging on to his chute by one hand thousands of feet above Eloy, Arizona.

Yee-haa!

JUST ASKING...

⭐ **Was the stunt for real?**
"It was carefully planned with many safety precautions. I had a harness under my clothes that was attached to the parachute and a modified parachute so I could release the main parachute and open the reserve. But in fact all went well, and I did climb back into the main parachute harness after the picture was taken."

⭐ **Is this the most dangerous thing you have ever done?**
"The most dangerous thing I ever did was to run with bulls in Spain. There were too many variables and things that could have gone wrong."

⭐ **What training do you need for your skydiving stunts?**
"The key is to assume that everything can and will go wrong. It is usually a series of small mistakes that put a skydiver into a dangerous situation."

No Pins Permitted

A labyrinth made of more than 20,000 balloons was installed in a shopping mall in Allaman, Switzerland. It took a team led by Didier Dvorak almost 200 hours to build the maze, which covered 263 square yards. Groups of four biodegradable balloons were attached to one another to form columns anchored by sandbags. The maze remained in place for 10 days.

To Boldly GO

Mythical Voyage

Oarsmen from various European countries gathered for a recreation of Jason's mythical quest for the Golden Fleece. A replica of the *Argo* set off on a two-month voyage from the Greek city of Volos to Venice, Italy, via the Corinth Canal. Luckily they didn't encounter the fire-breathing oxen, sleepless dragon, or crushing rocks that plagued Jason and his Argonauts.

Don't look down!

Bears with Altitude

Britain can claim a first in the space race as four teddies have taken a flight to an altitude of around 100,000 feet. Wearing spacesuits designed by students from local schools, the teddynauts were strapped to a weather balloon made by Cambridge University's Space Flight science club. The bears experienced temperatures of minus 31°F, before parachuting safely back to Earth.

Around the World in 13 Years

www.expedition360.com

Aberdeen

Jason Lewis was playing in a London band and running a cleaning company when a university friend suggested that they join forces for the journey of a lifetime—circumnavigating the globe using nothing but human power. The project, called Expedition 360, was intended to promote world citizenship and environmental responsibility, while raising funds for children's charities along the way. Although his friend left the expedition after five years, Jason continued, finishing his 46,505-mile trip at the Greenwich Meridian Line 13 years after setting off.

JUST ASKING...

Jason's top-five forms of transport

1. **Wooden boat** – across the Atlantic and Pacific oceans.
2. **Rollerblades** – across North America.
3. **Kayak** – from Australia to Singapore.
4. **Bicycle** – from Singapore to the Himalayas.
5. **Pedalo** – from Mumbai, India, across the Indian Ocean to Djibouti.

Jason's top-five "hiccups"

1. Struck by a car while Rollerblading across North America. Spent nine months recovering from two broken legs.
2. Attacked by a saltwater crocodile in Australia.
3. Arrested by Egyptian authorities on suspicion of spying. Later released.
4. Journey that was expected to take only 3 years took 13 and cost more than $400,000.
5. Suffered from malaria and septicemia.

Messing Around

Tofu Tossing

At an annual festival in China, tofu, or bean curd, is thrown to express best wishes and hope for a bumper harvest. Around 5,500 pounds of the stuff is flung during the event, and people believe that those who are most curd-covered will be happiest during the coming year.

Happy Spray Day

You may not agree, but in China the people who get wettest during the annual water-spray festival are said to be especially lucky. For the Dai people of Yunnan Province, the festival marks the start of their new year. It begins with a gentle sprinkling of water to express good wishes, but soon the super-soakers come out and everyone gets drenched.

Slippery Celebrations

In celebration of Indonesia's Independence Day, young people climb greased palm trees to reach prizes ranging from buckets to bicycles.

The tree trunks are so slippery that contestants need to stand on one another's shoulders.

Those who reach the top of the poles are expected to throw down prizes to share with the spectators beneath.

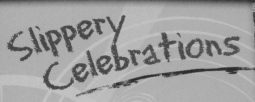

MIND BOGGLER!

FISH FLINGERS
Contestants at the annual Tunarama Festival in Australia compete to see how far they can throw a frozen tuna. For ecological and financial reasons, the fish have recently been replaced by plastic replicas.

Minty Madness

Students around the world have discovered that dropping a Mentos mint into a bottle of diet cola causes an eruption. But people in the Belgian city of Leuven decided to turn the party trick into a major event by launching 1,360 simultaneous 29-foot-high fountains. At least they wore plastic raincoats to shield themselves from the sticky soda shower.

It Must Be Love

Love Is in the Air

London advertising executive Johnny Skinner celebrated Valentine's Day by strapping himself to a chair 30 feet up, attached to a huge billboard. Johnny was entertained by a string quartet during the chilly three-hour wait for his girlfriend, Hannah Davies. When she finally arrived, he shouted, "I love you! Will you be my valentine?" Hannah said yes.

Wing-Walking Wedding

Woaaah!

The marriage of lovebirds Darren McWalters and Katie Hodgson got off to a flying start when they tied the knot 1,000 feet above the ground. The English couple flew alongside one another, balanced on identical biplanes, while fearless 67-year-old vicar George Brigham flew ahead, facing them. It was an especially big deal for the groom, who used to be afraid of heights!

Perfect Timing

Born in the year of the ox in the run-up to Valentine's Day, this calf has a perfect heart-shaped mark on his forehead. Japanese farmer Kazunori Yamazaki named the baby calf Ha-chan (meaning "heart") and hopes someone will buy him as a romantic gift, or that he will be adopted by a zoo or tourist farm.

MIND BOGGLER!

HOW DEEP IS YOUR LOVE?

Getting married 156 feet underground is unusual enough, but one wedding party at Howe Caverns in New York State made the day even more special by dressing as clowns.

Fairytale Wedding

British couple Mr. and Mrs. Green took the "green" theme to extremes when they married dressed as Shrek and Princess Fiona.

It took a makeup artist three hours to transform Keith Green and Christine England into the "gruesome twosome."

The bride couldn't persuade her son to dress up as Donkey, but other guests came dressed as characters from the film. Let's hope they live happily ogre after.

LEAP TO IT!
If you think this takes dressing up to extremes, check out the man who styles horses on page 120.

SHOCKING!

A man built up at least 30,000 volts of static electricity in his jacket simply by walking around the Australian city of Warrnambool, Victoria, in September 2005. Frank Clewer left a trail of scorch marks, carpet burns, and molten plastic behind him.

No Joke

A 26-year-old woman from Sydney, Australia, accidentally swallowed a teaspoon during a laughing fit while eating spaghetti. Doctors removed the six-inch spoon by lassoing the handle and pulling it upright before easing it out of her throat.

Lucky Survivor

Diver Eric Nerhus was saved by his weighted vest when a ten-foot great white shark swallowed his head and upper body and tried to bite him in half. Eric, who was searching for shellfish off the southeast coast of Australia, stabbed the shark in the face with his chisel until it let him go. He was rescued by a nearby boat and taken to the hospital with only chest injuries and a broken nose.

THIS S   WRITING MESSAGES

POST CARD
THIS SPACE FOR ADDRESS ONLY

PLACE
ONE CENT
STAMP
HERE

SAFARI

18300

On a Roll

Indian holy man Lotan Baba rolls his body along the ground for an average of 6 to 8 miles a day in a quest for world peace and salvation. He claims to have covered almost 20,000 miles. He once did penance for seven years by standing in one place and eating grass.

BIG BALL

A housepainter from Indiana has been applying coats of paint to a baseball since 1977. On dry days, Michael Carmichael can apply as many as ten new coats, and his original ball is now the size of a weather balloon. Mike got the idea back in the 1960s when he was playing baseball, and the ball accidentally fell into some paint.

GREECE

PAGE TURNER

Ninety-one-year-old Louise Brown from Scotland has borrowed more than 25,000 books from her local library, without a single fine for late returns. Mrs. Brown has been visiting the library for 60 years and has read almost every book on their shelves.

Birthday Suit

Luang Phoo Budda Thawaro celebrates his birthday by standing in front of the congregation at the Wat Krang Chu Si Charoensuk monastery, near Bangkok, Thailand, in a new orange robe — despite being dead since 1994. Each year the monks lift the former abbot's mummified body from a glass coffin and dress him in new clothes, then worshipers stick flakes of gold to his face.

HARD TO SWALLOW

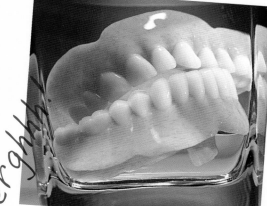

erghhh

A 38-year-old Romanian woman went to the hospital with stomach pains after accidentally swallowing her boyfriend's false teeth. X-rays revealed that the dentures were lodged in her stomach.

Keep at It

Home Sweet Home

A retired ice-cream seller has celebrated 100 years living in the same apartment. Alfonso De Marco moved to the property in Eastbourne, England, as a seven-year-old when his family arrived there from Italy. At the ripe old age of 107, he can still climb the stairs—perhaps thanks to all the ice cream he has eaten, suggests his daughter.

HINDU URDHABAHU

INDIA

RIPLEY'S ARCHIVE

HELD HIS ARMS ABOVE HIS HEAD FOR 20 YEARS

MIND BOGGLER!

NEVER GIVE UP
A 68-year-old South Korean woman is hoping to buy a truck, after finally passing her written driver's test on the 950th attempt! Cha-Sa-soon has been trying to pass the exam for four years.

Hands Up!

An Indian man named Urdhabahu held his arms above his head for 20 years.

Doctors say that, although this would be painful during the first three months, after that the arms would stay up because of loss of blood circulation and stiffening of the muscles.

42

Awesome Achievement

Hugo Vihlen has crossed the Atlantic in a boat little bigger than a bathtub, not once, but twice. Hugo's first voyage was in 1968, when he sailed from Morocco to Miami in a 5-foot-11-inch boat. When somebody else made the trip in an even smaller vessel in 1993, Hugo went one better and repeated his journey, risking 25-foot waves and pods of whales, in a boat just 5 feet 4½ inches long.

A Good Yarn

Women from the close-knit community of Mersham, England, have spent thousands of hours recreating their village in wool. The scale model consists of 100 items, including houses and gardens, cars, roads, and cricketers on the village green. The knitters met every week and it took about 23 years to complete.

Zzzzzz...

Don't Try This at Home

Taking the Plunge

Daredevil kayaker Pedro Olivia plunged 127 feet off the Salto Belo Falls in Brazil in a breath-taking freefall lasting 2.9 seconds. The 26-year-old Brazilian hit the water headfirst at 70 mph and surfaced behind the curtain of water, only to find a welcome party of boa constrictors. He emerged without a scratch—until he slipped on the rocks after climbing out.

Toy Racer

With just his feet as brakes, German speed demon Dirk Auer piloted a jet-powered toy car at speeds of up to 65 mph. The car's plastic shell was reinforced with carbon fiber and the wheels were replaced by those from a wheelchair, but the steering was original. The model aircraft engine heated up to 650°F and was nearly as loud as a Boeing 737.

MIND BOGGLER!

TRICK OR TREAT?

Inspired by Harry Houdini, Los Angeles escape artist Curtis Lovell II celebrated Halloween by being cuffed, shackled, and buried alive in a coffin covered with 200 pounds of dirt. Despite suffering swollen wrists and getting dirt in his eyes, he escaped within 16 minutes.

Phhhuuut

Head for Heights

Extreme balancing artist Eskil Ronningsbakken is never happier than when he's taking danger to new heights— be it perching on a cliff on a steel ring 3,000 feet above a fjord, riding a bicycle upside down across an icy ravine, or balancing on an ice cube suspended over a glacier. The Norwegian, who is in his thirties, has been practicing his death-defying skills since he was a child, after seeing an Indian yogi balancing on TV. Since then he has performed with circus troupes around the world.

JUST ASKING...

Why do you attempt these amazing performances?

"I have always been fascinated by people with extreme body control, and aim to show that anything is possible. It's about working hard, having a strong belief, and never giving up. I started training when I was five (I am now in my thirties), so balancing has become a major part of my life."

Which was your most difficult stunt?

"Performing upside down on top of a bike placed on a tightrope 3,000 feet high, in Kjerag, Norway, in 2005."

Picture Perfect

At just over 5 feet 4 inches tall and weighing 145 pounds, Joseph L. Greenstein might have been the kind of guy to get sand kicked in his face. But "The Mighty Atom" could bite nails in two, lift 470-pound weights with his teeth, and use his hair to bend an iron bar and hold back an airplane revving at 60 mph.

Headstand Hop

Just thinking about it may be enough to give you a headache, but Alexandre Patty, a 1930s entertainer, could bounce up and down a flight of stairs on his head. Even if you could do it, would you want to?

Tiny Titon

Walter Hudson weighed over 1,400 pounds before he died in 1991. His typical daily diet was two packs of sausages, a pound of bacon, 12 eggs, one loaf of bread, four hamburgers and four cheeseburgers, eight portions of French fries, three ham steaks, two chickens, four baked potatoes, four sweet potatoes, and four heads of broccoli.

Whopping Walter

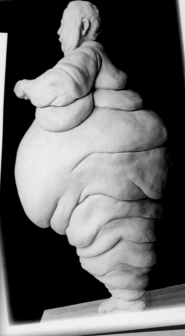

Human Unicorn

There have been several confirmed cases of humans growing horns. In 1696 an old woman even had her 12-inch horn removed and presented to the King of France. The horned man in this picture lived in China in the 1930s.

This tattooed man could save on laundry by going without a shirt. Although tattoos are common nowadays, in the 19th century they were so unusual that tattooed people could make a living appearing in sideshows. Heavily tattooed Charles Wagner earned $1,000 a week—a huge sum in the 1870s.

Non-iron Shirt

Look, No Hands

His dentist may not have approved, but mighty-jawed Jackie Del Rio from Chicago, Illinois, shown here lifting two tables and six chairs with his teeth, would have had no trouble getting a job with a moving company.

"This old world is a mighty interesting place ..."
Robert Ripley

Ball Games

Ball Control

Manoj Mishra of West Bengal, India, won a competition by balancing a soccer ball on his head for 14 hours.

According to the rules, the ball was not to be touched or moved during this period. The soccer fan, who performed yoga to keep still during his attempt, dedicated his victory to his hero, Argentinian soccer legend Diego Maradona.

Keepy-uppy King

Using his feet, thighs, chest, and head, professional freestyler Dan Magness kept a soccer ball in the air for 24 hours—that's more than four hours longer than anyone had achieved previously—touching the ball almost 250,000 times. The 25-year-old trained for 12 hours at a time over six weeks for this unusual marathon, which took place in central London.

Beach Ball Bash

Two three-story-high beach balls caused a stir when they were dropped from a building in downtown Dallas, Texas, onto a crowd of 2,500 people. Each ball was made from 4,085 square feet of standard beach-ball material and contained an inner balloon filled with helium to give it some lift. Even so, to push each ball required the strength of several adults and the desire of everyone to keep the balls rolling.

MIND BOGGLER!

STRETCH SNEAKER
It's every parent's dream—sneakers that grow with a child's feet. By pushing a button on the side, the shoes can be extended by one full size, which means half as many trips to the shoe store.

Anyone got a pin?

Ball with a Brain

Arguments with the referee could be a thing of the past now that Adidas has unveiled the intelligent soccer ball. A chip embedded in the ball uses a magnetic field to provide real-time feedback to a central computer, which tracks the ball on the field and sends the information directly to the referee, making it the most reliable and accurate soccer ball ever.

49

just 13 inches high!

LIMBO LEGEND

Aniket Chindak doesn't skate around parked cars, he rolls straight under them. The seven-year-old from Belgaum, southern India, was inspired to take up limbo-skating after seeing a girl skate under a car on TV. It took three months' practice to get his body into the right position, no higher than 8 inches from the ground. Now Aniket, who has been skating since he was 18 months old, trains for four hours a day and covers 60 miles each week. He has skated under 57 cars in 45 seconds, but his ambition is to build up his speed and skill so he can tackle a lineup of 100 cars.

In 2008, 55-year-old Dennis Walston, aka "King Limbo," bent over backward to squeeze his body under a bar just five-and-seven-eighths inches from the ground.

"The hardest thing is to go fast enough before I bend down," he says.

chapter three

Appliance of Science

School of Thought

Robo-prof

Have you ever wondered if your teachers are human? At a Japanese elementary school the answer could be no. A robot teacher called Saya is being tested at a school in Tokyo. She can take attendance, set tasks, answer questions, and thanks to motors in her face can also show surprise, fear, disgust, happiness, sadness—and she can show pride in her students, too.

Power Pack

Hiking in the great outdoors used to be about getting back to nature.

These days some of us rely so much on our gadgets that the idea of being a few yards from a power socket can seem like a step too far.

The answer lies in this voltaic backpack, which can charge your cell phone, MP3 player, hair appliances, and even your laptop, however far you get from civilization.

LEAP TO IT!
Turn the page to see how virtual beings can get even closer to home.

That's One Big Bag

You're not supposed to carry a bag heavier than 20 percent of your body weight. To wear this giant 143-pound backpack, seen on display at a shopping mall in Bangalore, India, you would need to weigh 715 pounds—and that's before you put anything in it. You would also need to be at least 50 feet tall, because it measures 25 by 9 feet.

PRIDE OF INDIA
KARNATAKA, BANGALORE & JAYANAGAR
WORLD'S BIGGEST SCHOOL BAG
Presented & Made by
Darshan - Modista
THE JAYANAGAR TRADERS ASSOCIATION

Working Lunch

Sometimes office workers just don't have the time or energy to leave their cubicles to heat up their lunch. The Heinz company has created a mini-microwave that can be plugged into a PC or laptop's USB port. So if you're hungry while completing an assignment and a handy sandwich seems too cold, the Beanzawave may be the answer.

...Ping!

Domestic Science

Eggs-actly Right

If you ask ten people how to cook a boiled egg, you may receive ten different answers. However, experts at the British Egg Information Service have now found a foolproof way to guarantee perfection every time. As the egg starts to cook, a high-tech, temperature-sensitive ink turns black to show whether it's soft, medium, or hard-boiled.

Soft

Pedal Power

Exercise bikes are great for keeping in shape. But what if you could convert your energy into electricity? A gym in Hong Kong is already harnessing people-power from its exercise machines to keep the lights glowing. It's possible to generate enough electricity to power an MP3 player or TV as you pedal.

POWER PLAY

A British student has designed a seesaw he hopes will provide power for schools in Africa. Five minutes' play could generate enough electricity to light a classroom.

Virtual Valet

He may remind you of the Magic Mirror in *Shrek*, but the Virtual Butler is designed to remind you of your appointments, announce when guests arrive, and control security cameras, doors, and gates. The "butler" will make announcements through your home speakers in an English accent, but unfortunately won't iron the newspapers or serve afternoon tea.

QUICK CHANGE

★ A virtual mirror has been designed for those who hate undressing to try on new clothes. Customers stand in front of the screen wearing a green T-shirt, which is replaced by their chosen garments.

Starry Night

Woaaah!

Sleep under the stars without leaving the comfort of your own bedroom. StarMurals are invisible by day, but at night your ceiling is transformed into a galaxy of twinkling stars, all hand-painted using a secret formula. If you'd like to drift into a deep sleep in deep space, your personalized universe can also include nebulae, comets, and meteor showers.

What Are the Chances?

Kitemare

Kiteboarders keep an eye out for sharks, dolphins, jellyfish, and even crocodiles, but David Sheridan never expected to get whacked by a whale. The 42-year-old Australian was 300 feet off the coast of New South Wales when a Southern Right Whale, swimming a few feet beneath him, smacked him on the back of the head with its tail.

Oooops!

Too Much to Swallow

Aircraft engines are designed to cope with swallowing the occasional unfortunate bird. But a baggage container proved too much for this Japanese jet, which was about to take off from the Los Angeles airport. Passengers were evacuated after one of the jet's engines sucked the empty container off a baggage cart that had been driven too close to the plane.

Wild Ride

I'm a pepper

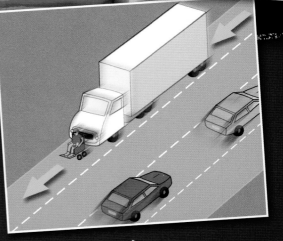

Ben Carpenter of Michigan had the ride of his life when the handles of his wheelchair became snagged in the front grille of a truck.

Ben had been crossing the road when the traffic light turned green and the truck moved forward. Horrified drivers dialed 911 as the rig roared down the highway at speeds up to 50 mph. The unaware driver couldn't believe it when the police caught up with him and his unwilling passenger four miles down the road. Although Ben lost the rubber from his wheelchair tires, fortunately he was unharmed.

CleverCars

Dream Machine

Olaf Mooij is the brains behind this wacky car. During the day, the car uses three cameras to record its surroundings as it drives. At night, it "dreams" by projecting the images from its travels inside its white transparent brain. Olaf, a Dutch artist, is well-known for his car art—his previous works include cars wearing wigs and a fossilized car.

Cool!

Fly Drive

Is it a car? Is it a plane? Motorists stuck in traffic may fantasize about taking to the skies, but now the dream has become a reality. The Terrafugia Transition Flying Car fits in a normal garage and runs on unleaded fuel. The two-seater's 27-foot wings unfold in 15 seconds, and it has a top air speed of 130 mph.

Weird Wheels

This car, named the "Oval Runner," won the prize in the automobile section of the Mitsubishi Motor's Fuso idea grand prize held in Kawasaki, Japan, in 1996. The oval-shaped wheels meant that the car could be driven in any direction, whichever way it was facing.

It might have been handy for parking, but it never caught on.

Green and Mean

Race cars are normally anything but eco-friendly. However, the WorldFirst Formula 3 car developed at England's Warwick University has excellent green credentials. Powered by biodiesel fuel produced from local chocolate waste, the car has a steering wheel made from a carrot-based material, a flax-fiber-and-soybean-oil foam seat, and rearview mirrors incorporating potato starch. And it can still reach 125 mph around corners.

The BIG Picture

SNOW TWO ALIKE

Snowflakes form when the water vapor in clouds freezes. They begin life as simple hexagonal prisms, but as they grow, they sprout branches that form more complex shapes. No two are alike because they grow at different rates, creating unique patterns depending on the temperature and humidity. Kenneth Libbrecht, professor of physics at the California Institute of Technology, has studied snowflakes for over ten years, and has captured their beauty using a specially designed photo-microscope. He picked up the snow crystals from a collection board using an artist's

JUST 0.8 inches HIGH

paintbrush and placed them on glass slides before photographing them. All the work took place outside in sub-zero temperatures, so the camera had to be placed inside a heated box to keep it functioning.

Grave News

Out of Time

Archaeologists have discovered what is thought to be a 100-year-old watch in an ancient Chinese tomb that was thought to have been sealed for 400 years. The baffling miniature timepiece is in the shape of a ring and has the word "Swiss" on the back. It was found encrusted in mud and rock, and the time had stopped at 10:06 a.m.

MIND BOGGLER!

SPOOKY SPOT
Residents of Indian Meadows and Shady Grove, Alabama, whose communities are partly built above Cherokee burial grounds, report seeing figures and hearing footsteps and scratching. In one house, a crying man's face appeared on several doors.

Phantom Photo

An eerie apparition in period clothing has been photographed peering out a crumbling window at Tantallon Castle in Scotland. Experts have confirmed that the image has not been digitally altered in any way. This is the second ghostly photo to have been shot at the ruined 14th-century fortress. A family snapshot taken 32 years earlier shows what appears to be a mysterious woman at a window.

Creepy...

Geeky Ghost

Ken Webster first noticed strange goings-on in his cottage near Chester, England, in 1984, when furniture was upended, tools disappeared, and cans were stacked in pyramids. When he borrowed a computer (in the days before the Internet), messages appeared on the screen in 17th-century English, signed "Thomas Harden." Two years later, Thomas said onscreen that he was leaving the area, and all the paranormal activity stopped.

Not So Hot

There are many mysteries surrounding the life of Nefertiti, a queen of ancient Egypt, but she has always been known for her beauty. Now German researchers have used CT scanning to uncover a secret within the famous, 3,300-year-old bust of the queen. Hidden inside is a detailed stone carving of her face, showing wrinkles, creases around her mouth, and a bump on her nose.

65

Call a Doctor!

Gross!

Head Case

When Aaron Dallas developed painful lumps on his head, he visited a doctor. At first he was diagnosed with an infected fly bite, then with shingles, but the lumps would not heal. One day, the Colorado man felt them moving. He returned to the doctor, who removed five botfly larvae. The eggs were probably deposited on his skin by a mosquito during a trip to Belize.

Seedling Surprise

When Justin Martin was involved in a vehicle rollover accident and thrown out the window into a pasture, he suffered a badly injured left arm and numerous broken bones. After four operations, he noticed a painful lump on his left arm. He returned to the hospital, where doctors removed a cocklebur plant, complete with a stem and bloom, from his arm.

COCKLEBUR

★ Cockleburs are invasive weeds that produce small seeds covered with strong, hooked spines. The seeds and seedlings are poisonous to animals.

Feeling Queasy?

Gag...

This tangle of giant roundworms was found in the intestines of a child from Kenya. The worm begins life when an egg hatches in the host's intestine. The larva then travels to the lungs via the blood vessels, where it continues to develop until it is coughed up and swallowed. Back in the small intestine, the worm, which infects around 1.2 billion people worldwide, completes its life cycle.

MIND BOGGLER!

MYSTERIOUS GROWTH
Russian surgeons thought that Artyom Sidorkin had a tumor in his lung, but instead they discovered a tiny fir tree. They assume that he had inhaled a seed, which germinated inside his lung.

Horned Humans

The book *Anomalies and Curiosities of Medicine* reports many cases of humans with horns, including a woman with 185 small horns and a 17th-century French woman who shed long horns from her forehead, one of which was presented to the king. This 88-year-old man from China has a curved horn.

Lost in Space

A group of cheesemakers from the west of England marked the 40th anniversary of the Moon landing by launching a wedge of Cheddar into the upper atmosphere. The giant leap for "cheesekind" ended in disappointment, however, when the GPS satellite system failed, and they lost track of the balloon carrying the cheese.

Wobbly Webs

Two spiders named Anita and Arabella joined astronauts aboard the Skylab space station as part of an experiment to study the effects of weightlessness on their webs. Their first efforts were sloppy and uneven, but as the spiders became acclimated, their webs became more accomplished, just like the ones they spin on Earth.

Space Hopper

Wojtek Czyz was a promising young soccer player until an accident on the field led to the loss of his lower leg. He has since gone on to represent Germany at the Paralympics, winning gold medals for long jump and 100 and 200 meters, thanks to an artificial leg made from an especially strong and light material developed for use on the International Space Station.

Kr. 1,50
FOREVISES PÅ FORLANGENDE

Cosmic Bubble

This may look like a super-sized soap bubble, but it is actually a planetary nebula. Nebulae are formed when aging stars eject their outer layers as glowing clouds of gas. Named the Soap Bubble Nebula, this rare phenomenon was first spotted by an amateur astronomer.

Long-Distance Wedding

A life-size cardboard cutout stood in for the groom when Yekaterina Dmitriyeva married Yuri Malenchenko in Houston, Texas. The Russian cosmonaut could not be there in person, because he was some 240 miles above the Earth aboard the International Space Station. Up in orbit, the real Yuri wore a bow tie with his space suit, and the newlyweds blew one another a kiss via a video link.

UFO MYSTERY

In 1967, Stefan Michalak from Winnipeg, Canada, was prospecting near Falcon Lake, Manitoba, when he claims to have seen two glowing, disk-shaped objects descend from the sky. When he approached one of the UFOs, a blast of hot gas shot out from a gridlike exhaust, setting his shirt on fire and causing burns to his chest in a similar grid pattern. He never learned what the UFOs actually were.

PERMANENT PRINTS

According to NASA, because there is no wind or rain on the Moon, the footprints left by astronauts will be there for a million years.

Star-Spangled Sky

On a clear, dark night the sky is dotted with countless stars, but we can only see those in a tiny area of our own galaxy, the Milky Way. Even under perfect conditions, just 1,100,000,000,000,000,000th (one hundred thousand trillionth) of the stars in the universe are visible from Earth.

69

Scene from Afar

Fantastic Photos

The Southern Alberta, Canada, Balloon Launch may not have looked impressive, but the spectacular images of the Earth's surface taken during the two-and-a-half-hour flight certainly were. The "do-it-yourself" device consisted of an ordinary digital camera strapped to a helium balloon, which reached an altitude of 117,585 feet. An onboard transmitter enabled its creator, Tony Rafaat, to retrieve the camera on landing.

3.11.2007 12:10

Giant Jellyfish

The image of a huge jellyfish mysteriously appeared in a field of barley in Oxfordshire, England. The 600-foot Portuguese man-of-war was about three times the size of typical crop circles, which started appearing in the English countryside in the 1970s. Originally thought to have been caused by UFOs, the patterns are now believed to be the work of artists who design them on computers.

10

Across the Pond

In May 2008, a giant drill bit appeared near Tower Bridge, London, England. A few days later, it was replaced by a contraption made of brass and wood. Then a similar device appeared near the Brooklyn Bridge in New York City. They were Telectroscopes, created by artist Paul St. George.

According to Paul, he was inspired by his (fictional) great-grandfather, who planned to dig a tunnel through the Earth.

Paul's tunnel was virtual, however, with video cameras at either end, allowing people in both cities to interact with one another.

LEAP TO IT!
Take a look at page 34 to discover which furry creatures made it to the stratosphere.

What they saw!

Techno Transport

One-Wheeled Wonder

In the early 1920s Davide Cislaghi, a former electrician, showed off his motorized monowheel in Milan, Italy. He was said to be as proud as a peacock as he drove for dozens of miles at speeds of up to 40 mph. The monowheel was steered by leaning from side to side, and the "steering wheel" itself was just something to hold on to.

Yee-haa

Bizarre Bike

It was a trip to smog-ridden Beijing, China, that inspired MIT freshman Ben Gulak to design a zero-emissions, all-electric motorbike. He decided to reduce the actual, as well as the carbon, footprint by moving the rear wheel next to the front. The side-by-side wheels are positioned directly beneath the rider, who leans forward to accelerate, as he would on a Segway.

Amazing Arachnids

Japan's no stranger to robots, but these 40-foot-tall, 37-ton giant spiders are stranger than most. Built by French performance art group La Machine, the robot spiders prowled the Yokohama waterfront to celebrate the 150th anniversary of the opening of the city's port. They are operated by 13 people and spout water from the front and back. Fog machines, lights, and music complete the effect.

MIND BOGGLER!

JAM BUSTER
Beat traffic jams with the Super Sky Cycle, a flying trike with fold-out rotor blades that can travel up to 70 mph in the air and 60 mph on the road.

Take to the Sky

Hovercrafts can be uncomfortable in bad weather, but Rudy Heeman's Hoverwing can take to the air if the waves suddenly get rough. The New Zealander spent 11 years and thousands of dollars designing the flying craft, which takes off at 60 mph and flies 6 feet above the water. He may not have full confidence in his invention yet, because he chose to test it close to a hospital!

chapter four

Super-Humans

Bionic Man

Arm Art

Two ears are not enough for Australian artist Stelios Arcadiou. He has had a third, artificial ear implanted on his arm and plans to attach a microphone to transmit what it is hearing over the Internet. In the past, he has attached a third artificial hand to one arm and swallowed a camera to explore the structure of his stomach.

MIND BOGGLER!

PLAYING AMAZING
A group at the University of New South Wales in Australia has created a robot that plays the clarinet, with human-like lips and tongue that vibrate the reed of the clarinet like any top musician would, and presses keys to produce the notes.

Finger Drive

A Finnish computer programmer is the only person in the world with a two-gigabyte finger. After losing half his ring finger in a motorbike accident, Jerry Jalava wanted a multifunction replacement. The "nail" of his prosthetic finger peels back to reveal a memory stick, so Jerry can detach his finger and plug it into the USB slot of his computer.

Eye-Cam

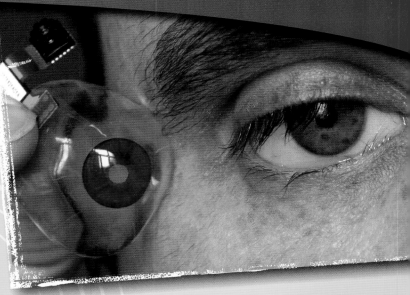

Rob Spence, who lost an eye following an accident, realized when he looked at his cell-phone camera that it was small enough to fit in his empty eye socket. The Canadian documentary filmmaker now plans to become a "human surveillance machine" with a camera concealed in his glass eye. His muscles will move the camera so it records exactly what he is seeing with his other eye.

Iron Man

After being paralyzed in an accident, Seiji Uchida was inspired during his recovery by a photo of the Matterhorn mountain in Switzerland. A motorized exoskeleton, worn by mountaineer Ken Noguchi, helped Seiji to realize his dream of climbing the mountain. The power of Ken's muscles was almost doubled by the suit, so he could give Seiji a piggyback up to the top.

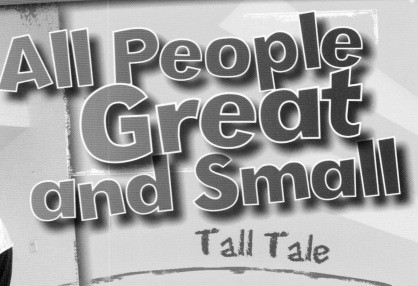

All People Great and Small

Tall Tale

When Zhao Liang, from Menan Province, China, needed a foot operation, hospital staff were stunned by his staggering size. The 27-year-old, who had to sleep on two beds placed end to end, measures almost 8 feet 1 inch tall. Weighing in at 341 pounds, Liang wears U.S. size 20 shoes, and his pants are the same height as his 5-foot-6-inch mother.

Bouncing Baby

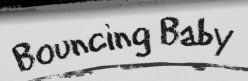

Born in 1936, this baby weighed 92 pounds at six months—the same as an average-sized 11-year-old and five times more than most babies that age.

Extreme Lengths

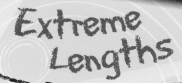

Despite owning a beauty parlor, Chenq Shiquin from Chongqing, China, has not had a haircut in 16 years. It takes her two hours to wash her 8-foot-long hair and another hour to comb it. However, Xie Quiping (left), also from China, had even longer locks—after growing her hair for more than 30 years it measured an incredible 18 feet 5 inches.

Little and Large

He Ping Ping, who stood just 29 inches tall, came face to knee with Svetlana Pankratova, whose legs alone are 52 inches long, in London, England, in 2009. Russian-born Svetlana, a former basketball player, is 6 feet 5 inches tall and also has large feet—a U.S. size 13. Ping Ping, from Inner Mongolia, China, was just the size of a man's palm when he was born, but sadly died in 2010.

AMMAZING APPETITE

Fyodor Makhnov, born in 1878, was known as "The Russian Giant." His average breakfast consisted of 20 eggs and 8 loaves of bread. For lunch, he had 5 pounds of meat and 2 pounds of potatoes, then in the evening he ate 5 pounds of meat, 3 loaves of bread, and some fruit, followed by a late-night snack of 15 eggs with another loaf of bread.

Lost Tooth

In 1978, teenager Doug Pritchard from Lenoir, North Carolina, went to the doctor with a sore foot, but maybe he should have gone to the dentist instead. The cause of his pain was a tooth growing in his instep.

Rare Reaction

Joanne Mackie from the West Midlands, England, discovered that she was allergic to her own baby when she developed blisters and a burning rash after giving birth. The rare condition affects just one in 50,000 pregnancies.

Long Sight

PARIS

A Norwegian man's transplanted cornea has been in use since 1885. The cornea was taken from the body of an elderly man and transplanted into Bernt Aune's right eye in 1958. At the time, the transplant was only expected to last for five years.

CONSTANT COUGH

Nicholas Peake has been coughing up to 100 times per hour for 15 years. The lecturer from England has coughed more than a million times since his problem first began. Nicholas, who has tried every known remedy, can control his coughing only by chewing gum — which he hates.

REMARKABLE RECOVERY

Two-year-old Oluchi Nwaubani made a complete recovery after spending nearly 20 minutes at the bottom of a London swimming pool. Normally the brain begins to shut down after six minutes without oxygen, and the heart stops after ten. Doctors believe she was saved by the cold water, which caused her body to go into a hibernation-like state.

NO H$_2$O

Ashleigh Morris cannot swim, take a bath, or go out in the rain. Even sweating makes her break out in a rash. The young woman from Melbourne, Australia, has been allergic to water since she was 14. She is only one of a handful of people in the world to suffer from the rare condition.

Retro Runner

Running backward is the way forward for Swiss runner Rinaldo Inabnit, who used a rearview mirror to run backward for seven miles up a mountain in the Alps. "People think we're not normal," said Rinaldo, "but we're simply using our bodies differently."

HOUSE HUSBAND

Mr. Stjepan Lizacic developed a passion for housework after receiving a transplanted kidney from a 50-year-old woman. His wife is delighted that the Croatian lumberjack now enjoys ironing, sewing, washing dishes, and even knitting.

A 11193 Byrå-bill

Forevises på forlangende

11194 Byrå-billett

Forevises på forlangende.

Family Matters

No Way!

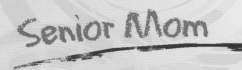

Seeing Double

Visitors to the village of Kodinhi, India, might do a double take and decide to get their eyes tested. With more than 220 sets of twins born to 2,000 families, the remote village in the Kerala region has nearly six times as many twins as the worldwide average. Experts have no explanation for the twin trend that has affected the village for the last 60 years.

Senior Mom

After being married for 55 years, Rajo Devi gave birth to her first child, a baby girl, at the age of 70.

Mrs. Devi is India's second 70-year-old mother. A few months earlier, twins were born to Omkari Panwar. As is common in rural India, neither woman has a birth certificate, so it's impossible to prove who is the older mother.

Three of a Kind

A mother is more likely to get struck by lightning than to give birth to three identical babies, so triplets Olivia, Gabriella, and Alessia Testa are particularly special. The girls were born in a hospital in Peterborough, England, where their mother works as a midwife.

New mothers of identical babies often paint their babies' toenails, or dress them in different colors, to tell them apart.

Triplets are likely to go through 10,000 diapers during their first year.

WHAT ARE THE ODDS?

★ The chance of giving birth to twins is 1 in 90, but for identical twins it's 1 in 285. The likelihood of giving birth to triplets is 1 in 8,100, but if they're identical, the odds soar to 1 in 5 million. Quadruplets make up only 1 in 729,000 births, and the odds of having identical quads is 1 in 13 million!

Beyond Belief

Coming or Going?

Raymond Gonzales freaks people out with his flexible feet. He has been able to turn them backward for as long as he can remember, and always assumed it was normal. The Iraq war veteran tried out the trick in front of his drill sergeant, who called him in. Raymond expected to be disciplined, but instead he was asked to demonstrate his skill to the other officers.

It's a Gas

Back in the 1930s, "Edema the human automobile tire" entertained crowds by inflating his stomach to three times its normal size using an ordinary tire pump. It may sound like a wacky idea, but today surgeons regularly inflate the abdomens of their patients to create a working space when performing certain types of surgery.

Twisted!

Believe It or Not!
by Ripley

HUMAN AUTOMOBILE TIRE!

EDEMA
IS INFLATED WITH AN ORDINARY AUTO PUMP
TO **THREE TIMES HIS NORMAL SIZE!**

NOW APPEARING IN THE ODDITORIUM

This Little Piggy...

This person might have trouble fitting into the latest designer footwear, but could easily count beyond 20 using their fingers and toes. Extra fingers and toes are not unusual, occurring in five babies in every 10,000. An eight-toed foot is rare, but a case of 12 digits on each hand and foot has been recorded.

Pint-Sized Powerhouse

At 20 years old, mini-muscleman Romeo Dev is 2 feet 9 inches tall and weighs just 21 pounds. Pictured here with his trainer Ranjeet Pal, Romeo has been pumping iron at his local gym in Phagwara, India, for two years, using dumbbells one-sixth his weight. Apart from weightlifting, Romeo likes to keep fit by doing aerobics and dancing.

MIND BOGGLER!

MEDICAL MYSTERY

Doctors are baffled by an Australian woman who is blind for three days out of every six, when her eyes involuntarily clamp shut and she cannot open them.

Er ER Please

No Laughing Matter

Lin Kong was using a four-inch pair of scissors as a toothpick when a friend made him laugh, and the scissors slipped down his throat. Doctors in Putian, China, had to remove them using only a local anesthetic because a general anesthetic would have relaxed his throat muscles, allowing the scissors to fall still further into his esophagus.

Mind over Matter

Chinese Shaolin monks believe the mind can control the body. Here one monk lies on upturned knives with a double-sided nail bed on his stomach, while another monk lies on the nails. A concrete block is placed on the second monk's stomach, which a third monk hits with a hammer.

Metal Miscellany

The Glore Psychiatric Museum in Minnesota is home to a display of 1,446 items removed from the stomach and intestines of a former patient. She died during surgery from bleeding caused by the mound of metal, which included 453 nails, 42 screws, safety pins, hairpins, buttons, spoon tops, and salt and pepper shaker tops.

MIND BOGGLER!

BRAIN WORM
Doctors in Arizona thought their patient had a tumor deep in her brain, so they were delighted to discover a tapeworm instead of a cancerous growth.

Hairball Horror

When a U.S. teenager complained of stomach pains, vomiting, and weight loss, doctors performed a scan to untangle the mystery. They discovered that the girl's stomach was blocked by a mass of black, curly hair, which weighed 10 pounds and measured 15 inches by 7 inches by 7 inches. The 18-year-old admitted that she had been eating her hair for five years.

The BIG Picture

IN A BIND

This elderly Chinese woman's shoes are less than 4 inches long. When she was a child, in accordance with tradition, her four smaller toes were bent underneath the sole of her foot and her feet were tightly wrapped in bandages, forcing the arch of her foot upward. The practice of foot-binding began in China in the 10th century and it became a sign that a woman was wellborn and wealthy. The custom endured for over a thousand years before it was finally banned

The bound feet were difficult to keep clean and often became very smelly.

in 1911. Chinese men considered the tiny, pointed feet very attractive and it was often hard for a woman with normal feet to find a husband.

Guardian Angels

Saved by the Boots

Peter and Sally Bunbury were watching their prize dairy cows make their way into the milking parlor, when suddenly all 120 toppled like dominoes. Everything in the shed had become electrified after the main electricity cable was damaged by lightning, and the cows were all killed instantly. They had been felled by an 11,000-volt shock, but Peter and Sally survived unharmed, thanks to their rubber boots.

Hanging Around

This unfortunate driver was crossing Grand Marais, Minnesota, when his station wagon skidded on the icy road and crashed into a bridge wall. The impact was mighty enough to propel the vehicle's front section over the edge, leaving just the back to counter the weight and prevent the cab from plummeting to the river below. Although emergency services were quickly on the scene, it took four full hours before a smart strategy for rescue could be devised and the hapless driver rescued safely.

Jawsome Encounter

Hannah Mighall was surfing with her cousin off the coast of Tasmania, Australia, when a 16-foot great white shark latched on to her leg and dragged her under the water.

The man-eater took three bites from 13-year-old Hannah's leg and a big chunk out of her surfboard, before her brave cousin Syb Mundy managed to fight off the shark. Hannah needed more than 200 stitches in her leg and plans to hang her surfboard on her bedroom wall as a reminder of her lucky escape.

MIND BOGGLER!

COOL SURVIVORS
Two Myanmarese (Burmese) fishermen were rescued after being spotted floating in an icebox. The pair had survived for 25 days in shark-infested waters after their boat sank.

No Pain No Gain

Stinky Work

Dirty or cracked eggs used to be sniffed to sort the good from the bad. An experienced worker would break and smell 7,000 to 11,000 eggs a day.

TOP SMELLY JOBS

★ Soap was originally made by boiling up dead animals. The fat was skimmed from the top, then mixed with potash and boiled until soap formed at the top of the mixture.

★ The purple dye used for royal robes was made by soaking shellfish in urine until they rotted.

★ Turning animal hides into leather was a revolting process. Urine was rubbed into the animal skin to remove the hair, then the hide was tanned by rubbing it with dung.

Un-bee-lievable

Buzzzz...

The "bee-man" show was the highlight of the annual honey festival held in Kaohsiung County, Taiwan. Six beekeepers, including 80-year-old Chuang Hsi-ching, got up close and personal with several million bees. Each "bee-man" attracted up to 600,000 bees from 106 hives. The bees crawled all over their bodies, leaving just their faces bee-free.

Chili Champ

After munching her way through 51 of the world's hottest chilies in two minutes, Indian mother Anandita Dutta Tamuly went on to smear the seeds of 24 of the red-hot peppers in her eyes.

Anandita, from the Assam region of India, has been chomping on chilies since she was five years old.

Pucker Up

Zhang Cunying won the chance to buy a Chevrolet for only one yuan (12 cents) after kissing it for more than 24 hours. In the contest, six cars were lined up in a Beijing, China, mall, and 120 competitors had to kiss them without touching the cars with any other part of their bodies. When just 28 people remained, the organizers made them balance on one foot with their hands behind their backs to make the contest harder.

Who's Driving?

Tiny Two-Wheeler

"Circus Boy" Bobby Hunt is not especially tall, but he's still a bit big for his bike. The tiny bicycle is 7¾ inches high and 3 inches long, with Rollerblade wheels cut down to the size of silver dollars. Bobby can fit only two toes on the miniature pedals, but he's still able to pop a no-handed wheelie.

Steering by Sound

People might say you need eyes in the back of your head to drive on India's busy city streets, but O.P. Sharma chose to ride his motorcycle through heavy traffic in Ludhiana completely blindfolded. The magician said he was guided by his sensitive hearing and hypnotism. Meanwhile, brave pedestrians offered him sweets and placed garlands around his neck.

Look out!

Blind Ambition

Larry Woody lost his sight after an accident, but the former race-car driver and pit-crew technician didn't lose his love of cars. Larry opened his own repair shop in Oregon and still works as a mechanic, using his hands and ears instead of his eyes. He drives race cars with the help of a passenger and hopes to break the land-speed record for a blind person.

LEAP TO IT!
Could the blindfolded motorcyclist avoid the invisible car? Can you spot it on page 112?

Compact Car

British car fanatic Perry Watkins has converted a Postman Pat children's ride into a street-legal vehicle just 39 inches high and 26 inches wide.

Even after removing Pat and his black-and-white cat, 6-foot-tall Perry still has trouble getting into the tiny car, which is mounted on a mini quad bike. He plans to hit the road in the car on tours of Great Britain, Europe, and Australia.

chapter five

Artistic License

Coins & Cards

Presenting the President

Brick Obama

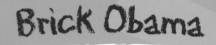

Over a thousand tiny faceless figures, each made of 30 to 40 bricks, assembled to witness the LEGO® inauguration of Barack Obama at LEGOland®, California. Celebrity guests, including Aretha Franklin, Yo-Yo Ma, and Oprah Winfrey, rubbed plastic shoulders with political dignitaries at the Carlsbad theme park. No detail was overlooked—there was even a line for the four portable restrooms.

Spitting Image

Artist Franz Spohn has created a six-foot-square portrait of President Obama made from 12,784 gumballs. More than 100 volunteers, who were instructed not to chew the art materials, helped position the gumballs in Ravenna, Ohio.

Purple was the most used color, followed by orange and blue.

The President joins Robert Ripley, Michael Jackson, Rosa Parks, and Dr. Martin Luther King, Jr., who have all been immortalized in gumballs.

Tooth Tats

U.S. dental technician Steve Heward is also a trained tattooist and has combined both skills to hand paint minute works of art onto tooth crowns. A tooth tattoo takes about half an hour to paint, and designs range from Abraham Lincoln and George Washington to Mickey Mouse and Elvis—but whatever the design, from a distance people might mistake it for a piece of spinach.

PAST PRESIDENTS

★ James Garfield was truly ambidextrous: He could write Latin with one hand while writing Greek with the other.

★ Thomas Jefferson is said to have invented the coat hanger, the hideaway bed, and the dumbwaiter.

★ Jimmy Carter is a speed reader and could at one time read more than 2,000 words a minute.

★ James Madison was 5 feet 6 inches tall, and his weight hardly ever exceeded 100 pounds.

★ Andrew Johnson never attended school and only learned to write at the age of 17.

Lincoln Likeness

Scott Blake's portrait of Abraham Lincoln was created from 42 images of U.S. presidents. The small images were arranged according to shade, so dark areas featured a president with a full head of dark hair and a dark tie, while a bald president with a white tie was used for the light areas.

According to the artist, Pixel President is about recycling information in an artistic way.

Big on Medium

Cubist Art

If completing the Rubik's Cube isn't enough of a challenge, try using the pesky puzzle to create art, such as this portrait made from hundreds of scrambled cubes. French street artist "Invader," known for installing mosaics of Space Invader characters in cities around the world, has turned the cubes into artworks. His works include images of the "Mona Lisa," Robert De Niro, and the Dalai Lama.

Tiger Eye

Sometimes, getting creative gets personal. Kurt Drake's canvas is his own face! And he's not alone: Many body painting artists come together every year at the World Bodypainting Festival to showcase their best work.

Light Graffiti

"Light writing" was demonstrated by Picasso almost 100 years ago. Now Lichtfaktor, an art group from Germany, has developed the technique to create moving images. Working at night, one of the group draws in the air with a flashlight, while another takes photographs using an exposure of at least 20 seconds to capture the trail of light. Images are then combined on a computer. Why not try it yourself?

LEAP TO IT!
Find out how to re-CYCLE cardboard boxes on page 111.

Coffee Canvas

Coffee geeks express their creative side by drawing designs in the foamed milk of lattes and cappuccinos. The standard pattern is the fernlike "rosetta," made by rocking the milk pitcher back and forth. Now inventor Oleksiy Pikalo has produced a machine to take latte art to a new level by printing on the milk froth using edible ink.

Eat Your Art Out

Man Machine

We have heard about Japanese robots that replace pets, companions, and even fashion models, but a machine at London's Victoria station reverses this trend. Commuters using the Human Vending Machine might think that the face they see in the glass is a reflection, but the machine's gadgetry has been replaced by a real humanoid who hands customers their chocolate and chats with them.

MIND BOGGLER!

MODERN ART?
Coffee is the medium for Filipino artist Sunshine Plata's work. She produces shades of brown by mixing different quantities of coffee with water. Strangely, she prefers drinking tea.

Potato Heads

Have you ever picked up a potato and been reminded of someone? Lebanese artist Ginou Choueiri believes that potatoes have much in common with human faces because they come in different colors, shapes, and sizes and have porous skin, just like ours. Ginou has created almost 1,000 potato portraits, including Foo Fighters frontman Dave Grohl and former president George W. Bush.

anyone for fries?

All of a Quiver

San Francisco may be used to some ground tremors, but nothing compared to the wobbles felt in Liz Hickok's colorful recreation of the city in Jell-O. Liz makes a complete scale model first and then uses it to make molds for the Jell-O. A whole scene takes about three months to complete, and once made, is lit from underneath or behind, so the Jell-O glows.

As her artwork lasts just a week, Liz quickly takes a picture and then sits back as her city slowly slides onto the floor.

Small World

Tiny Ted

Bettina Kaminksi from Germany specializes in miniature needlecrafts and her motto is "the smaller, the better." So after making Mini-the-Pooh, a bear just 5 millimeters tall (under one-fifth of an inch), she created his baby brother, Micro Ted, who measures less than three and a half millimeters (just over one-eighth of an inch). Both bears are hand-stitched and have jointed arms and legs.

Nano-ball Needed

Scientists from Kaiserslautern University in Germany have used nanotechnology to create a microscopic soccer field. Measuring only 500 by 380 nanometers, it has all the details and markings of a full-sized field. Twenty thousand of the nano-fields could fit on the tip of a single human hair, and it can only be viewed using a powerful electron microscope.

Titchy pitchy

Mini-meals

Gail Tucker and her mother, Aileen, specialize in making models of English food one-twelfth the normal size. Ranging from Tudor delicacies, such as baby eels in broth or a platter of tripe, to modern-day cakes, the tiny dishes take about three days to make. Some of the details, such as fruit seeds, are painted with the help of a magnifying glass and are invisible to the naked eye.

Bite-Sized Burger

Photographer Nadia Caffesse has found a way to help her fellow Texans lose weight. While a typical burger is about 5 inches in diameter, this miniature version is only about an inch wide. Nadia and her husband made all the items for this downsized fast-food feast, which they later shared, including the tiny home-baked bun, and the tray and soda cup.

The BIG Picture

Father-of-two Robert Bradford glanced into a box of his children's broken and discarded toys one day and was inspired by the great combination of jumbled colors, shapes, and textures. The artist from Cornwall, south-west England, decided to bring new life to the old toys by transforming them into large-scale sculptures. His first piece was an Alsatian dog, made from his own children's toys, but since then he has had to source his materials from yard sales and thrift stores. Now his creations, which can contain up to 3,000 toys, sell for up to $20,000.

Some critics say that his sculptures are rubbish—and the artist has to agree that this is perfectly true!

Big Shots

In 2008, a giant photomontage went on display in Birmingham, England. People from the surrounding area had submitted 112,896 photos relating to their daily lives to create "The Big Picture." The main image in this 100-foot-square mosaic is a photograph of amateur boxer Arthur James Bunce, taken in 1926 and sent in by his granddaughter Lucy Moore.

Waldo on the Web

Fans of Waldo can now seek him out on Google Earth. Canadian artist Melanie Coles has installed a 55-foot painting of the geeky character on a rooftop in Vancouver. Waldo spotters will have to wait for Google to update its images of the area before they can locate his perch. Melanie hopes other people will follow her lead and create a worldwide network of web Waldos.

Giant Gulliver

A park in Taiwan played host to a 196-foot-long figure of Gulliver with a hole in his foot, so visitors could enter his body and explore his organs. Thousands of people learned about anatomy as they walked alongside bones the size of telegraph poles, mazelike intestines, teeth the size of pillows, and nostrils as big as soccer balls, while a hidden generator blew air out of the lungs.

Mammoth Muskrat

Constructed from wood, wire, and thatch, this giant muskrat was installed in Zuid, Holland, to mark the country's lowest point below sea level. Artist Florentijn Hofman chose the rodent because muskrats damage the dikes and levees that protect the country from flooding.

The size of the animal is intended to show that it is a huge threat to the low-lying land.

109

Paper Glut

Page Turner

It's sometimes said that the birth of the Internet—and more recently the e-book—means the death of the traditional book, but old books are being given new life thanks to Brian Dettmer. Like a surgeon doing an autopsy, the American artist uses clamps, scalpels, and tweezers to dissect a book and reveal its insides. Selected words and pictures are exposed, forming a 3-D sculpture, but nothing extra is added and none of the pages are moved or changed.

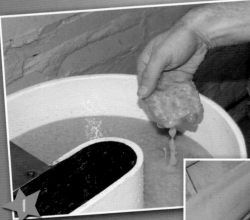

Fibers from the sheep droppings are mixed with other recycled pulps.

Special sieves are used to form the pulp into sheets.

Waste Not, Want Not

The sheets are pressed to remove the water, then hung up to dry.

It's an idea not to be sniffed at. Creative Paper Wales, UK, has won a business award by making handcrafted paper and cards using recycled paper, rags... and sheep droppings. Sheep digest only 50 percent of what they eat, so when the droppings are washed and sterilized, cellulose fibers remain. These are mixed to form paper and cardboard, while the leftover water is used as liquid fertilizer.

Extreme Recycling

While most people discard cardboard boxes into dumpsters, Chris Gilmour takes them out and puts them to good use.

The British artist makes full-sized models using nothing more than cardboard and glue. His detailed replicas range from motor vehicles, including James Bond's Aston Martin complete with ejector seat and machine guns, to musical instruments. His bicycles even have cardboard spokes and chains, and his dentist's chair comes with a cardboard drill.

Fortun
RED

Hide and Seek

Neat!

Vanishing Act

Sara Watson could be forgiven for forgetting where she parked her car. The British art student has spray-painted this Skoda Fabia so it merges perfectly with its surroundings. It took three weeks to transform the car, which was donated by a company that recycles old vehicles. Sara was pleased to report that several people have since bumped into her invisible car.

Seabed Statues

Divers and snorkelers enjoying the warm, clear waters of Grenada may be surprised to come across a circle of life-sized figures standing on the seabed. Created by English artist Jason Taylor, the underwater sculpture park is designed to celebrate Caribbean culture and encourage marine life. The statues are already covered in algae and provide a home for shrimps, octopuses, and moray eels.

LEAP TO IT! Take a look at page 131 to see what happened when an unlucky bunny met a hungry heron.

Now You See It...

The Rolling Stone is a mobile living module built from environmentally friendly materials. The surface is made from recycled aluminum tiles, so it reflects its surroundings and blends into the landscape. There is a bedroom, a bathroom, and a living room with a kitchenette. A reservoir on top collects rainwater, and each unit comes equipped with a solar-power system or wind turbine mounted on top.

Clear View

When artist-turned-medical-student Satre Stuelk found himself with access to a CT scanner, he decided to combine art and science and put it to creative use. Satre has given everyday objects from a toaster to a Barbie doll the CT treatment. Once he has scanned the objects, Satre processes them on his home computer and retouches the images.

BACK TO SCHOOL

Fifty years after David Ingham was expelled from Ermysted's Grammar School, in Yorkshire, England, he was invited back—to paint a portrait of the headmaster who had thrown him out. Headmaster Marcelus "Bru" Forster told the young David he wouldn't amount to anything, but the former pupil proved him wrong by becoming an art teacher.

Against the Tide

Before Andres Amador starts work, he checks the tide tables and picks up his rake. His canvas is the beach close to his San Francisco home, where he creates huge patterns of spirals and symbols. Unfortunately, the ocean has no respect for his skill. Soon after he has completed his intricate designs, they are washed away by the incoming tide.

Branching Out

Instead of drawing trees, Tim Knowles lets the trees draw for themselves. The British artist attaches pens to their branches and positions a canvas beside or below them. As the wind blows, the movement of the branches creates patterns on the canvas.

Hi-yo Silver!

A 10-foot-tall silver horse made from 5,000 CDs went on display as part of a recycled sculpture show at HorseWorld, an equine-welfare charity near Bristol, England. Its creator, Dean Williams, said he knew the horse would be in good hands, even if it slipped a disk!

Kr. 0.75
Forevises på forlangende
London, Eng.

FRANCE TRAVEL

J 615
J 61560

114

Hand-Painted

Italian artist Mario Mariotti, who died in 1997, always had a canvas at hand. He could turn his hands into all kinds of fantastic creatures, including animals, athletes, and musicians, just by bending his fingers and adding some paint and a few props.

dirty work

Living on an unpaved back road means Scott Wade's car is usually covered in dust. But rather than head for the car wash, the graphic artist reaches for his brushes. His recreations of old masters, drawn in the dirt on his rear windshield, only last until the next cloudburst, but a trip around the block soon provides him with another blank canvas.

Good Enough to Eat

A closer look at Carl Warner's landscapes reveals that they are created entirely from vegetables, meat, fish, and dairy products. The British photographer's "Foodscapes" include coconut haystacks, forests of broccoli and celery, seas of smoked salmon and cabbage, and mountains of bread with potato rocks.

THIS SPACE FOR WRITING MESSAGES

POST

THIS SPACE FOR

It's Choc O'clock

Italian artist Angelo Feduzzi sculpted a 35-foot-high model of London's Big Ben clock tower entirely from chocolate. The scale model was the highlight of a Christmas food festival in central Italy. It took two weeks to put together, and the cold winter temperatures ensured that it didn't melt during the week-long event.

Fine Figures

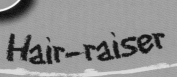Hair-raiser

When Eric Hahn from Nebraska saw a 24-inch Mohawk hairstyle on a TV show, he knew he could top that—and having grown his hair for seven years, he had the assets to rise to the challenge. Eric's Mohawk measured an incredible 27 inches, and he raised more than $850 for a local charity and Locks of Love, a group that collects hair to make wigs for cancer patients.

Body Art

Geoff Ostling, from Sydney, Australia, allowed his whole body to become a canvas for artist Ex de Merci, covering his body with all the flowers of a Sydney garden. A retired teacher, Geoff didn't get his first tattoo until he was in his forties, and has plans to donate his skin to the National Gallery in Canberra, Australia, when he dies.

Clip Art

Even the most enthusiastic recycler might think twice about reusing nail clippings, but these body by-products can become works of art. Just think how long it would take to collect enough to create this elephant made from nails. More recently, California artist Tim Hawkinson took nail art to another dimension by constructing a two-inch bird skeleton from his own nail clippings.

Car-osaurus

Indian artist Jitish Kallat was inspired to make Collidonthus when he saw a wrecked car on his way to work. It looks like a dinosaur skeleton, but it is actually made from fiberglass copies of bones from various animals. This is Jitish's second skeletal sculpture. His first, Autosaurus Tripous, was a recreation of an auto-rickshaw. The bone-based vehicles represent the chaos of Mumbai, India's busy streets.

Boneshaker

Critter Kingdom

Looking Good

Mane Event

My Little Pony would have been jealous of this well-groomed horse as it received star treatment from celebrity hairdresser Acacio da Silva.

Three ponies took part in a photo shoot by Julian Wolkenstein, posing in curls, bangs, and dreadlocks.

It took four hours to attach and style each horse's hair extensions, and the resulting 'dos could have been undone in seconds if they'd tossed their heads.

Purple Pete

Teachers and pupils were amazed to see a purple squirrel outside their classroom in southern England. Although experts were baffled, the school's registrar thinks she may have the answer. "Pete," as he has been named, has been seen going into a building where old computers are stored and could have been chewing on printer-ink cartridges, then grooming his fur.

Frightful Feline

The name says it all. "Ugly Bat Boy" is one ugly cat.

He has a tangle of hair on his chest, a wrinkled face, bald, rubbery skin, and a ratlike tail.

Vet Stephen Barrett adopted "Uggs," as he is known, as a kitten, and he has lived at the New Hampshire veterinary hospital for the past eight years. "He does look odd, but he's a lovely natured cat," said Dr. Barrett.

Grrrrr!

Horsing Around

German designer Hildegard Bergbauer, who makes traditional Bavarian dirndl dresses, remembers watching shows where animals appeared on stage wearing clothes with hats and handbags. So she decided to adapt her designs for cats, dogs, and even horses. In case dirndl dresses are too girly, the designer also makes lederhosen—cowhide shorts with leather suspenders—for pets.

LEAP TO IT!
Go to page 131 to see another unusual picture of a German animal.

What's Normal?

Nosy Bunny

This dwarf rabbit should be able to sniff out a tasty carrot twice as fast as its litter mates.

The baby bunny with two noses was discovered among a delivery of six-week-old rabbits at a Connecticut pet store.

Staff have grown attached to the remarkable rabbit, who looks doubly cute when he twitches his nose.

MIND BOGGLER!

16TH CENTURY MOLLUSK
A clam, plucked from the sea north of Iceland, was estimated to be 405 to 410 years old.

Supermom Sheep

A sheep often gives birth to twins, and triplets are quite common, but a ewe in Xuchang, China, has produced an extraordinary brood of six lambs. While lamb sextuplets are rare enough, there have been several recorded cases of sheep giving birth to seven. Ewes do not usually have enough milk for such a large family, so some lambs have to be fostered or hand-fed.

Big Bull

Chilli puts the rest of his herd in the shade. This Friesian bull weighs well over a ton and is as big as a small elephant. As a six-day-old calf, he was left on the doorstep of the Ferne Animal Sanctuary in Somerset, England. Nine years later, he measures 6 foot 6 inches to the top of his shoulders—18 inches more than the average Friesian.

Spot the Difference

Three-year-old Button, whose father appeared in the film *102 Dalmatians*, gave birth to 18 puppies just one year after having a litter of 16. The average number is just eight or nine. Six nurses were on hand to look after the puppies when they were delivered by Caesarean section. Button's owners, from Leicestershire, England, had to work round the clock to help feed the giant litter.

Man's Best Friends

Proud Penguin

Nils Olav, a 3-foot-tall penguin who lives at Edinburgh Zoo in Scotland, has already been made honorary colonel-in-chief of the Norwegian king's guard, and now he has also been given a knighthood! Nils was touched by the king's sword on both shoulders, and a badge symbolizing his knighthood was attached to his flipper. King penguins from the zoo have served as mascots for the Norwegian army since the 1970s.

Snail Trail

It may be an odd ambition, but schoolgirl Tiana Walton from Cheshire, England, was delighted to achieve a personal best when she allowed 25 snails to slither across her face. The nine-year-old animal lover said she found it relaxing, but the snails were a bit cold and smelly, and she could see their big, long eyes looking at her.

Yuk!

Doggy Diaper

House training a puppy can take six months, and that's a lot of puddles—and worse. Diapers may save your floors, but it's difficult to keep them on your pet. Dorrie Krenkel, who grew tired of diapers falling off of her chihuahua, invented this harness. It works with standard babies' diapers, and all you have to do is poke a hole for your dog's tail.

MIND BOGGLER!

BIG PET
During World War II in England a woman hid a baby elephant in her back garden so it could escape the air raids.

Live-in Llama

Pets come in all shapes and sizes but not many people would want to share their apartment with a 300-pound llama. Nicole Doepper from Germany has cared for Socke since he lost part of his hind leg at birth. Now Nicole is looking for a mate for the three-year-old llama, in the hope that he can be persuaded to leave home.

H2...oh

Daring Rescue

When a 375-pound male black bear wandered into a Florida beachfront neighborhood, wildlife-conservation officers fired a tranquilizer dart at the animal. The bear bolted into the sea to try to escape, but the drug started to take effect, and he was in danger of drowning. Brave biologist Adam Warwick jumped in and saved the animal, who was later relocated to the Osceola National Forest.

Bottoms Up

Patrons at an English pub may think they've had one too many when they spot Aussie—a goldfish that has been swimming upside down for the past four years. Aussie, who has become a local tourist attraction, shares a tank with Eddie, who swims normally. Their owner says that Aussie seems quite happy—as far as anyone can tell.

FLIPPING FISH

Fish that swim upside down usually have problems with their swim bladders, which keep them balanced in the water. Aussie could have inherited the condition from her parents, or she may just need more vegetables in her diet.

Wet 'n' Wild

Cats are supposed to hate water, but white Bengal tiger Odin is a big exception to the rule.

Odin was hand-raised at Six Flags Discovery Kingdom Zoo near San Francisco, California, and learned to swim by diving in after chunks of meat. A glass-fronted tank has been built so visitors can watch him gliding through the water. White tigers get their color from an unusual combination of genes and are rare. Only a dozen have been seen in the wild over the past 100 years.

The BIG Picture

GECKO GRIP

These photos, taken through a microscope, reveal the secret of a gecko's gravity-defying grip. The little lizards can run up polished glass walls and upside down across ceilings thanks to their hairy feet. The millions of tiny hairs produce an electrical attraction that acts like glue. As it walks, the gecko rolls the hairs onto the surface, then peels them off again.

Close Encounters

Pushmi-pullyu

These conjoined twin calves were born in Kentucky in 1932. They each had four legs and complete bodies, but they were joined together at the rear.

Conjoined twins occur in all animals, but they are rare, making up about only one in 100,000 births.

Catdog

Cassia Aparecida de Souza from Brazil claims that her cat Mimi gave birth to puppies after mating with the dog next door. Mimi apparently had a litter of six—three kittens and three puppies. The kittens died, but Mimi continued to nurse the puppies. Scientists are skeptical and suggest that, as Mimi gave birth in a field, she may have adopted some orphaned pups.

Horse Hybrid

Is it a zebra? Is it a horse? It's a zorse! Eclyse lives at a safari park in northern Germany. Her dad was a zebra stallion, and her mom was a horse. Horses and zebras are often crossbred in Africa where the strong animals are used for trekking. When the father is a horse and the mother is a zebra, their offspring is called a horbra or hebra.

MIND BOGGLER!

ELEPHANTS BEE-WARE?

Elephants dislike bees, especially if they come close to their sensitive trunks, so recordings of angry bees are being used in African countries to keep elephants away from valuable crops.

What a Catch!

Herons normally eat fish, but when this hungry heron spotted a baby rabbit emerging from a hole, it swooped down and grabbed it by the ears, then swallowed it whole. Gray herons, which have an average wingspan of six feet, have become common in Holland, where this picture was taken. They are moving into towns and even turn up at zoos at feeding time.

Mommy!

Behave Yourself

Reduce, Reuse, Recycle

When Brian Williams' wife cut his hair, she threw the trimmings into the backyard, but they didn't lie on the ground for long. The couple, from Barnstaple, England, were astonished to see birds collecting the cut hair to line their nests. First a robin, then a goldfinch, followed by a greenfinch, swooped down to pick up the retired teacher's leftover locks.

Cat burglar

Feline Felon

Instead of chasing mice, Henry the cat hunts socks. This cat burglar regularly comes home with a sock in his mouth and his owner, Louise Brandon, from Loughborough, England, now has a large bagful. She has no idea where he's getting them from and has appealed to her neighbors to come forward if socks are disappearing from their clotheslines.

STOP THE PRESS

Henry's haul so far...
- ★ 85 socks
- ★ a pair of underpants
- ★ several gloves

Cat Cam

Mr. Lee, a tomcat from South Carolina, can never escape his owner Jurgen Perthold's watchful eye after he was fully equipped with a camera, also known as "Cat Cam." In 2005 Perthold decided to put a 2-ounce camera around Mr. Lee's neck that takes an image an hour for 48 hours, to document his encounters exploring garages, with snakes, cats, and even his girlfriend!

Please Return to:

Thank you!

Tough Luck

More than a Mouthful

A catfish bit off more than it could chew when it tried to eat a basketball. Bill Driver spotted the fish in Sandalwood Lake, Kansas, and waded in to remove the ball, but it was stuck. His wife brought a knife, and they deflated the ball so they could take it out. The 50-pound fish seemed unharmed and headed off for the deepest part of the lake.

Gone with the Wind

When a storm struck a flea market in Waterford Township, Michigan, all kinds of things were swept up in the strong winds, including Dorothy and Lavern Utley's 5-pound chihuahua, Tinkerbell. After searching for their missing dog for two days, the Utleys enlisted the help of a pet psychic who directed them to a wooded field a half a mile away, where they found their puppy.

Car Cocoon

Imagine returning to your parked car to find it wrapped in a silk cocoon. This is what happened to a motorist in Spuikade, Holland. Millions of caterpillars had crawled onto the vehicle after stripping the leaves from nearby trees. They were the larvae of spindle ermine moths, which spin silk cocoons to protect themselves from predators.

MIND BOGGLER!

EXTRA INGREDIENT
An Australian doctor cracked open a chicken's egg and found a dead gecko inside. He believes the gecko may have climbed inside the chicken during the egg-making process.

Pop Goes the Hedgehog

A veterinary nurse had to pop a hedgehog who had swelled up like a balloon. Michelin, as he was named, had a rare condition in which air from his lungs built up under his skin. When he arrived at the Wildlife Aid Centre in Leatherhead, England, the nurse carefully made a hole in his skin, and three hours later he was back to his normal size.

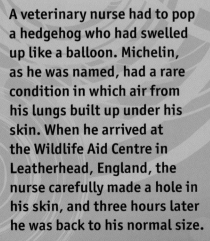

Streeetch...

Fish Net

When Hurricane Ike struck West Orange, Texas, in September 2008, it caused a storm surge that carried large numbers of fish inland. When the flood waters receded, thousands of fish were stranded on the road, and some were found stuck headfirst in a chain-link fence.

Ancient Cetacean

A bowhead whale caught off the coast of Alaska in 2007 was found to have a harpoon point dating from around 1880 embedded in its neck. Experts estimate that the 50-ton whale must have been about 130 years old. Bowheads are an endangered species, and there are now just 8,000 to 12,000 left in the world.

Bomber Birds

Australian magpies defend their territories during the breeding season by swooping down and attacking passersby. Because the birds are less likely to attack if people are looking at them, pedestrians are advised to get "eyes in the backs of their heads" by drawing or sewing eyes on the backs of their hats, or wearing sunglasses back to front.

Wish You Were Here!

Double-take

Staff at a veterinary clinic in Perth, Australia, were amazed when a cat gave birth to a kitten with two faces. The kitten had a cleft palate on one side, so could eat only with one mouth, but both mouths could meow simultaneously. The male kitten had two normal litter mates.

Hippo Home

In 2000, a South African couple had to get used to looking after a hippo, when they took in baby Jessica the Hippo, after she had been swept away from her mother in devastating floods. Only a few hours old, Jessica still had her umbilical cord attached and weighed only 35 pounds when they found her on the banks of a river in Limpopo Province. They gave her heavy-duty massages and allowed her to wander the house until she started breaking the beds. Now weighing one-ton, Jessica has left home but still eats some of her 175 pounds of food a day there.

PINK PLAGUE

In 2004, vacationers on Fuerteventura in the Canary Islands fled from the beaches when a 100-million-strong swarm of pink locusts descended from the sky. The three-inch-long insects, which can eat their own body weight each day, had devoured two-and-a-half-million acres of crops in Mauritania, Africa, before crossing the Atlantic.

Fluorescent Fish

Bioengineered pets could be coming to an aquarium near you. A company in Taiwan has created glow-in-the-dark fish by injecting a fluorescent protein from jellyfish into the eggs of Japanese rice fish.

Back Seat Drivers

Petrifying Passenger

When a Texas highway patrol officer stopped a man on suspicion of making an illegal U-turn, he was shocked to find a 6-foot alligator lounging in the back of the car. Along with his reptilian passenger, motorist William Johnson was also found to be carrying stolen goods. He was handed over to the local police, while the gator was handed over to a local game warden.

Tusk Force

Tourists on safari hope to get a good view of wildlife, but this Swiss pair's encounter was too close for comfort. Rico Beltrame and his sister Angela attracted the attention of this 6-ton elephant when they were visiting the Hluhluwe Umfolozi nature reserve in South Africa. The elephant leaned on their car for about five minutes before wandering off.

Look out!

Horseback Rider

When Hieronim Kapuscinski bought a 260-pound foal at a Polish livestock market, he forgot he didn't have a horse trailer. Hieronim removed the rear seat from his tiny Fiat Uno car and crammed the horse in the back, while he and his two friends squeezed in the front. Police caught up with him when the car broke down and fined him $100 for inappropriate use of a vehicle.

MIND BOGGLER!

SUV STOWAWAY
A cat survived a 70-mile ride down the New Jersey Turnpike in the underbelly of an SUV unharmed, apart from burned paws, singed fur, and a missing claw.

Parading Parakeet

Musician Barbara Schenker regularly rides around east London on her bike carrying her parakeet Sammy in his own customized, see-through backpack. She is training the bird to follow in the footprints of his superstar predecessors, Sammy and Sammy II, who have whistled the national anthem to Queen Elizabeth II and appeared on TV.

Index

PHOTO CREDITS: Ripley Entertainment Inc. and the editors of this book wish to thank the following photographers, agents and other individuals for permission to use and reprint the following photographs in this book. Any photographs included in this book that are not acknowledged below are property of the Ripley Archives. Great effort has been made to obtain permission from the owners of all material included in this book. Any errors that may have been made are unintentional and will gladly be corrected in future printings if notice is sent to Ripley Entertainment Inc., 7576 Kingspointe Parkway, Suite 188, Orlando, Florida 32819.

COVER/TITLE PAGE: Photo copyright ©René Hoff with permission of makeup artist/model Kurt Drake from Wolfe Face Art & FX and the World Bodypainting Festival, Seeboden

BACK COVER: Top left-Carnival Cruise Lines; Bottom left-B. Hunt; Middle right-Plane crash hotel—Allan Templeton

COVER BACKGROUND: James Bowyer/iStockphoto

CONTENTS PAGE: 3: Tiny bike—B. Hunt; Parachute formation—Keith Macbeth; Miniscule bears—www.minatura.co.uk; Legs backward—Ray Gonzales

INTRO PAGES: 6: Tiny burger and chips—Wenn; Car made from toy car—Andy Willsheer/Rex Features; 8-toed feet—©UPPA/Photoshot; **7:** Shrek wedding couple—SWNS.com

CHAPTER 1: 9: Plane crash hotel—Allan Templeton; **10:** Colorful iceberg—Steve Nicol Australian Antarctic Division; Natural rock formation—Gavin Bernard/Barcroft Media Ltd; **11:** Birth of a new island—Fredrik Fransson; **12:** Extreme Scrabble—Barcroft Media Ltd; Mind boggler—©Joshua Blake/iStock.com; Watching *Titanic* in boats—Chris Jackson/Getty Images Europe; **13:** Plane crash hotel—Allan Templeton; Gold pagoda on rock—Reuters/Aung Hia Tun; **14:** Upside down house—Sean Gallup/Getty Images; Mind boggler—©Joshua Blake/iStock.com; Optical illusion building—J Griffin Stewart: www.jgriffinstewart.com; **15:** Leaning German church—Reuters/Staff Photographer; **16:** Monster motorbike—Solent News/Rex Features; Bike covered in crystals—Wenn; **17:** Penny farthing man—Joff Summerfield; Tiny bike—B. Hunt; Bike with multi-angled wheel—ChinaFotoPress/Photocome/Press Association Images; **18–19:** Alphabet from space—Wenn; **20:** Truck with sticks—Wenn; Car on bike—Wenn; **21:** Baskets on bike—Lois Raimondo/AP/Press Association Images; Assistive limb robot—Olivier Maire/AP/Press Association Images; Train in Pakistan—Khalid Tanveer/AP/Press Association Images; **22:** Electricity potato statues—Wenn; Bottle monastery—Bronek Kaminski/Barcroft Media Ltd; **23:** Man who collected waste—Leon Chameides; **24:** Worms—iStock.com; **24–25:** Masking tape notes—©Dar Yang Yan/iStock.com; Speech messages—iStock.com; **25:** Portugal postcard—iStock.com; Tickets—©Russell Tate/iStock.com; Sticky note—iStock.com; Dinosaur—©Allan Tooley/iStock.com; **26:** Man eating lizards—Reuters/Sukree Sukplang; **27:** Roasted rats—Reuters/China Photos; Moldy sandwich bags—www.thinkofthe.com Sherwood Forlee; Green egg—Krunoslav Petric/24sata/Pixsell/Press Association Images; **28:** Sit down coffin—Camera Press; Golf course funeral home—Wenn; **29:** Glow in the dark tombstone—www.fuerrot.at/Rex Features; Urn—©Paul Bodea/Fotolia.com; Ashes to art—Caters News

CHAPTER 2: 31: Parachute formation—Keith Macbeth; **32:** Piano on hot air balloon—Kerstin Wendt/DPA/Press Association Images; Parachute formation—Keith Macbeth; **33:** Parachutist—Joe Jennings/Barcroft Media; Balloon labyrinth—Reuters/Valentin Flauraud; **34:** Rowers in Corinth Canal—Aris Messinis/Getty Images; Teddies in space—Geoffrey Robinson/Rex Features; **35:** Jason Lewis' boat trip—Sebastian Meyer/Stringer/Getty Images; **36:** Bean curd fighting—Wenn; Water pistols—ChinaFotoPress/Photocome/Press Association Images; **37:** Greasy pole climbing—Sipa Press/Rex Features; Mind boggler—©Joshua Blake/iStock.com; Soda spray festival—AFP/Getty Images; **38:** Valentine man—David Parry/PA Archive/Press Association Images; Married on bi-planes—Barry Batchelor/PA Archive/Press Association Images; **39:** Cow with heart marking—Itsuo Inouye/AP/Press Association Images; Mind boggler—©Joshua Blake/iStock.com; Shrek wedding—SWNS.com; Horse hairdos—Barcroft Media Ltd; **40:** Spoon—©Sergejs Razvodovskis/iStock.com; Vintage postcard—©Kevin Russ/iStock.com; Tons of tickets—©Russell Tate/iStock.com; **40–41:** Nine travel stickers—©Kathy Konkle/iStock.com; Notes with masking tape—©Dar Yang Yan/iStock.com; **41:** Lined paper—iStock.com; False teeth—©Hengfen Li/iStock.com; **42:** Living in the same flat for 100 years—M & Y Agency Ltd/Rex Features; Mind boggler—©Joshua Blake/iStock.com; **43:** Hugo Vilhen crossing Atlantic—Keith Botfield; Knitting a village—Gareth Fuller/PA Wire/Press Association Images; **44:** Kayaking over waterfall—Ben Stookesberry/Barcroft Media Ltd; Mind boggler—©Joshua Blake/iStock.com; Extreme skating—Action Press/Rex Features; **45:** Balancing man—Sindre Lundvold/Barcroft Media Ltd; **48:** Balancing ball on head—©EuroPics [CEN]; Keepy uppy—Johnny Green/PA Wire/Press Association Images; **49:** Big beach ball—Carvinal Cruiselines; Mind boggler—©Joshua Blake/iStock.com; Clever football—Rex Features; **50–51:** Limbo boy—Simon De Trey-White/Barcroft Media Ltd

CHAPTER 3: 53: Uno motorcycle—Glenn Roberts, Motorcycle Mojo Magazine (www.motorcyclemojo.com); **54:** Robotic teacher—Reuters/Issei Kato; Solar powered backpack—Barcroft Media Ltd; **55:** Giant backpack—Indranil Mukherjee/Getty Images; Virtual butler—www.opulent-items.com/Barcroft Media; Mini microwave—Jennifer Fairhurst/PA Video/Press Association Images; **56:** Perfect egg—Rex Features; Pedal washing machines—Reuters/Reinhard Krause; **57:** Virtual butler—www.opulent-items.com/Barcroft Media; Stars mural—Rex Features; **58:** Surfer on whale—Newspix/David Sheridan/Rex Features; Container in jet—Reuters/STR New; **59:** Wheelchair ride—AP/Press Association Images; **60:** Brain car—Wenn; Flying car—Terrafugia/Rex Features; **61:** Oval wheels—Reuters/Kimimasa Mayama; Chocolate fuelled car—University of Warwick; **62–63:** Snowflakes—Kenneth Librecht/Barcroft Media Ltd; **64:** Swiss watch—©EuroPics [CEN]; Mind boggler—©Joshua Blake/iStock.com; Face in castle—Wenn; **65:** Face of Neferiti—Wenn; **66:** Single botfly—NHPA/Photoshot; Botfly in head—Kelley Cox/AP/Press Association Images; Justin Martin's plant—Justin Bruce Martin; **67:** Worms in stomach—CDC/Science Photo Library; Mind boggler—©Joshua Blake/iStock.com; Horn on head—ChinaFotoPress/Wang Zi/Photocome/Press Association Images; **68:** Thunderbird badge—Rocket Design; Bubble nebula—N.S. WIYN,NOAO,AURA,NAF/Rex Features; **68–69:** Notes with masking tape—©Dar Yang Yan/iStock.com; Tons of tickets—©Russell Tate/iStock.com; **69:** Paris postcard—©Marisa Allegra Williams/iStock.com; Lined paper—iStock.com; Adhesive notes—©Yunus Arakon/iStock.com; Aim high dream big—iStock.com; **70:** Balloon view from space—Tony Rafaat/ Barcroft Media Ltd; Balloon into space—Carl Gill/Barcroft Media Ltd; Jellyfish crop circles—M&Y Agency Ltd/Rex Features; **71:** Tunnel under the Atlantic—Cate Gillon/Getty Images; Teddies in space—Geoffrey Robinson/Rex Features; **72:** One-wheeler—PA/PA Archive/Press Association Images; Uno motorcycle—Glenn Roberts, Motorcycle Mojo Magazine (www.motorcyclemojo.com); **73:** Mechanical spider—Nippon News/Barcroft Media Ltd; Mind boggler—©Joshua Blake/iStock.com; Hovercraft—BP/Barcroft Media Ltd

CHAPTER 4: 75: Tiny bike—B. Hunt; **76:** Ear on arm—David Cheskin/PA Wire/Press Association Images; Mind boggler—©Joshua Blake/iStock.com; USB finger—Reuters/Attila Cser; **77:** Prosthetic eye—Reuters/Yves Herman; Assistive limb robot—Olivier Marie/AP/Press Association Images; **78:** Tallest man—Reuters/China Daily China Daily Information Corp/CDIC; **79:** Longest hair—Top Photo Group/Rex Features; Ping Ping and woman with long legs—Jean/Jean/Empics Entertainment; **80:** Eyeball—©Olena Druzhynina/istock.com; Notes with masking tape—©Dar Yang Yan/iStock.com; **80–81:** Nine travel stickers—©Kathy Konkle/iStock.com; **81:** Lined paper—iStock.com; House husband—©Eric Hood/iStock.com; Old bath—©Greg Nicholas/iStock.com; Yellow sticky note—iStock.com; Adhesive notes—©Yunus Arakon/iStock.com; Tons of tickets—©Russell Tate/iStock.com; **82:** Village of twins—Niklas Halle'n/Barcroft Media Ltd; Old mother—Simon De Trey-White/Bl/Barcroft Media Ltd; **83:** Identical triplets—MEN Media; **84:** Backward legs—Ray Gonzales; **85:** 8-toed feet—©UPPA/Photoshot; Mind boggler—©Joshua Blake/iStock.com; Small body builder—Simon De Trey-White/Barcroft Media Ltd; **86:** X-ray scissors in throat—©EuroPics [CEN]; Shaolin Monks—Joe Klamar/Getty Images; **87:** Stomach contents—Courtesy of Glore Psychiatric Museum; Mind boggler—©Joshua Blake/iStock.com; Hairball—Wenn; **88–89:** Bound feet in shoes—China Photos/Getty Images; **89:** Bound feet—Mark Ralston/Getty Images; **90:** Lightning strikes cows—Richard Austin/Rex Features; Van over lake—Wenn; **91:** Shark attacked surfboard—L Winburn/Newspix/Rex Features; Mind boggler—©Joshua Blake/iStock.com; **92:** Covered in bees—Barcroft Media; **93:** Chilli in eyes—AP/Press Association Images; Kissing the car marathon—Reuters/John Gress; **94:** Tiny bike—B. Hunt; Blind motorcyclist—Reuters/Stringer India; **95:** Blind mechanic—Brian Davies/AP/Press Association Images; Invisible car—Barcroft Pacific/Barcroft Media Ltd; Car made from toy car—Andy Willsheer/Rex Features

CHAPTER 5: 97: Painting with lasers—Lichtfaktor; **98:** Lego White House inauguration—Reuters/Mike Blake; **99:** Tooth art—Steven Heward; Barcode art—Scott Blake barcodeart.com; **100:** Photo copyright ©René Hoff with permission of makeup artist/model Kurt Drake from Wolfe Face Art & FX and the World Bodypainting Festival, Seeboden; Rubik's cube art—Wenn; **101:** Painting with lasers—Lichtfaktor; Cardboard bike—Courtesy Pergui Artecontemporanea, photo Marco De Palma; Cappuccino art—GB/Barcroft Media Ltd; **102:** Human vending machine—Ian Nicholson/PA Archive/Press Association Images; Mind boggler—©Joshua Blake/iStock.com; Potato portraits—Ginou Choueiri/Rex Features; **103:** Jelly art San Francisco—Elizabeth Hickok; **104:** Mind boggler—©Joshua Blake/iStock.com; Miniscule bears—www.minatura.co.uk; Microscopic football pitch—Wenn; **105:** Model meals—Gary Roberts/Rex Features; Tiny burger and chips—Wenn; **106–107:** Toy dog—Robert Bradford/Barcroft Media Ltd; **108:** Boxer made of photos—Photograph of Tipton born Arthur James Bunce taken in 1926 shared by his granddaughter Lucy; Giant where's waldo—Emiliano Sepulveda; **109:** Giant Gulliver—Reuters/Staff Photographer; Thatched art—Wenn; **110:** Book carvings—Image courtesy of the Artists and Packer Schopf Gallery; Sheep poo paper—www.creativepaperwales.co.uk; **111:** Cardboard art—Courtesy Pergui Artecontemporanea, photo Marco De Palma; **112:** Invisible car—Barcroft Pacific/Barcroft Media Ltd; Underwater sculpture—Wenn; **113:** Blend into background caravan—Wenn; Pelican eating rabbit—©UPPA/Photoshot; X-ray bunny—Satre Stuelke radiologyart.com; **114:** Lined paper—iStock.com; Tons of tickets—©Russell Tate/iStock.com; Adhesive notes—©Yunus Arakon/iStock.com; Nine travel stickers—©Kathy Konkle/iStock.com; **114–115:** Beach in Mexico—©Roberto A Sanchez/iStock.com; **115:** Notes with masking tape—©Dar Yang Yan/iStock.com; Vintage postcard—©Kevin Russ/iStock.com; Chocolate bar—©Stephanie DeLay/iStock.com; Lined paper—iStock.com; **116:** Big Mohican—Wenn; Tattooed man—Lisa Maree Williams/Getty Images; **117:** Mind boggler—©Joshua Blake/iStock.com; Bone car—Reuters/B Mathur

CHAPTER 6: 119: Odin the tiger—Rick Murphy, Six Flags Discovery Kingdom; **120:** Horse hairdos—Barcroft Media Ltd; Purple squirrel—Zachary Culpin/Rex Features; **121:** Ugly cat—Barcroft Media Ltd; Horses in dresses—Reuters/Alexandra Beier; Zorse—Reuters/Ho New; **122:** Two nostril rabbit—Barry Bland/Barcroft Media Ltd; Mind boggler—©Joshua Blake/iStock.com; six lambs—ChinaFotoPress/Photocome/Press Association Images; **123:** Chilli the massive cow—Ferne Animal Sanctuary; 33 puppies in one litter—Geoffrey Robinson/Rex Features; **124:** Knighted penguin—Rex Features; Snails on face—Andrew Price/Rex Features; **125:** Dog with nappy—Wenn; Mind boggler—©Joshua Blake/iStock.com; Living with llamas—Reuters/Ina Fassbender; **126:** Bear rescue—Wenn; Upside-down fish—SWNS.com; **127:** Odin the tiger—Rick Murphy, Six Flags Discovery Kingdom; **128–129:** Gecko foot—Cheryl Power/Science Photo Library; Green gecko—©swisshippo/fotolia.com; **130:** Cat/dog mixed offspring—Reuters/Stringer Brazil; **131:** Zorse—Reuters/Ho New; Mind boggler—©Joshua Blake/iStock.com; Pelican eating rabbit—©UPPA/Photoshot; **132:** Bird makes pensioner's hair nest—SWNS.com; Cat brings in socks—SWNS.com; **133:** Cat cam—Mr Lee/J. Perthold; **134:** Blown away dog—Mark Hicks/AP/Press Association Images; **135:** Car covered in moths—©UPPA/Photoshot; Mind boggler—©Joshua Blake/iStock.com; Popped hedgehog—Wenn; **136:** Herring—©Nikolay Suslov/iStock.com; Lined paper—iStock.com; Keys—iStock.com; Portugal postcard—iStock.com; Vintage tickets—iStock.com; **137:** 1940s postcard—©Alex Mathers/iStock.com; Yellow smiley face—©Mike Matas/iStock.com; Desert locust—©Eric Isselée/iStock.com; Yellow sticky note—iStock.com; **138:** Alligator in car—Splash news; Elephant on car— Zoom/Barcroft Media Ltd; **139:** Horse on back seat—©EuroPics [CEN];Mind boggler—©Joshua Blake/iStock.com; Budgie on moped—Rosie Hallam/Barcroft Media Ltd